#50

W9-BJL-517

THE SERENITY PRAYER

God, grant us the serenity

To accept the things we cannot change,

Courage to change the things we can,

And wisdom to know the difference.

FIRST EDITION PUBLISHED IN 1991
SECOND EDITION PUBLISHED IN 1992
THIRD EDITION PUBLISHED IN 1996

The adaptation of the Serenity Prayer and the Reflections printed by permission of Dr. Patrick J. Carnes.

The Twelve Steps and Twelve Traditions of Alcoholics Anonymous, How It Works and The Promises are reprinted and adapted by permission of Alcoholics Anonymous World Service, Inc.

Tools of Recovery are reprinted and adapted by permission of Workaholics Anonymous.

RCA Conference Approved Literature.

This book was printed in the United States of America with soy ink on recycled paper.

ISBN 0-9637495-2-8

CONTENTS

INTRODUCTION

Recovering Couples Anonymous (RCA) was founded in the Fall of 1988. In the short time since the first groups formed in Minnesota and California, and later merged, RCA has grown to become an international fellowship that has meetings all over the United States as well as in many countries around the world.

Since the second edition of the *Recovering Couples Anonymous* was published in August, 1992, there has been an enormous amount of growth in the fellowship. 67 new meetings have been started, 1565 copies of *Recovering Couples Anonymous* have been sold, hundreds of couples have attended the RCA international conventions, and the World Service Office has received thousands of request for information regarding the fellowship.

The third edition of the *Recovering Couples Anonymous* has incorporated new literature that has been developed since 1992, such as the expanded versions of the 12-Step guide and the 12 Traditions. In order to reduce the printing costs and therefore reduce the cost of *Recovering Couples Anonymous*, we have reformatted the book so it can be printed as a quality paper back. This makes the third edition more bookstore/bookshelf friendly. It is our hope and goal that *Recovering Couples Anonymous* will become more widely available in bookstores throughout the country.

As stated in the introduction to the first edition, "We are all pioneers in the movement. Many of us are starting groups in areas where there is little support for our needs. In these struggles we hope that there will come a strength forged out of the energy that we see cropping up all over the world as new meetings form, and as our fellowship continues to grow."

This book is dedicated to all the couples who are still suffering.

1997

PREFACE

Who We Are

We are couples committed to restoring healthy communication, caring, and greater intimacy to our relationships. We suffer from many addictions and co-addictions; some identified and some not, some treated and some not. We also come from different levels of brokenness. Many of us have been separated or near divorce. Some of us are new in our relationships and seek to build intimacy as we grow together as couples.

Our History

Recovering Couples Anonymous (RCA) was founded in the fall of 1988 in Minneapolis, Minnesota. Several couples completed a "We Came To Believe" seminar which focused on working the 12 Steps in relationships. Groups were formed independently in California at about the same time, which later merged with the Minnesota group to form RCA. These couples discovered over time that the same 12 Steps that had helped them recover from different addictions individually also helped to build the health of their relationships.

Our Steps, Traditions, and Principles are based on and adapted from those of Alcoholics Anonymous. The Minneapolis fellowship revised the 12 Steps, 12 Traditions, How It Works, and The Promises to reflect couples' language and issues. They also developed a meeting guide and a list of the characteristics of dysfunctional and functional couples.

RCA groups can be found in cities throughout the world. Member group meetings are listed in the International Meeting Directory.

The World Service Organization (WSO) serves as a connecting point for all groups and as a clearinghouse of new materials. The International Convention is held annually. WSO originated in Minnesota and is now located in St. Louis, Missouri.

Our Philosophy

RCA is a tool for recovery and not an end in itself. It exists to promote caring, communication and intimacy. A quite successful formula of RCA is my individual recovery plus your individual recovery plus our couple recovery equals a healthy recovering relationship.

We believe that a relationship, or coupleship, is like an infant, needing constant nurturing and care from both partners. It is important that each partner accept mutual responsibility for the problems and/or progress of the relationship, and furthermore, that each recognizes his/her individual recovery as an important factor for couple recovery.

We think of our lives in a relationship as being represented by a three-legged stool. Our individual recovery, our partner's recovery, and our relationship recovery are all important "legs" to the serenity, stability and intimacy we each seek.

The main theme and purpose of RCA is quite simple: couples need to treat their relationship together as an entity distinct and separate from their individual recoveries. This "entity" or relationship is like a little child who needs to be nurtured by its parents (the two members of the relationship) and has the same kind of nurturing and recovery needs as the individual. As couples we need meetings, sponsors, service, and a 12-Step program. We have couples serve as sponsors of other couples.

We define sobriety as the ability to remain in commitment to the relationship. We believe that this sobriety begins when we take the First Step together. That date for many of us has become like a second anniversary, our legal anniversary being the first. Slips or relapses occur when we question our commitment, refuse to accept mutual responsibility for our problems, get into blaming behavior, and/or stop working the program together.

Usually we will know when slips occur because we become distant from our partner, going into that land of ESCAPE or numbness in the variety of ways we have probably known since childhood. This distance may lead to slips in our individual recovery as we revert to old ways of coping with our loneliness. Slips in our individual addictions affect our relationships, obviously, but may not be slips in couple recovery if we are honest about them with our partner and admit our personal responsibility for them.

Who May Come?

The only requirement for membership in RCA is that you are a couple seeking to restore a caring, committed and intimate relationship.

Ultimately, we feel it is important for both members of a couple to be involved in individual recovery for real progress to be made in the relationship. It is not, however, a requirement to get started in couple recovery. RCA is a safe place to begin that healing process and offers support for continued individual work.

Each member of the couple needs to take responsibility for the dysfunction of the relationship. We do not seek to blame our partner. Our partners may have chosen to medicate the pain of their loneliness with various addictions. We do not seek to take responsibility for those. As two people, however, we both bring family-of-origin messages, abuse experiences, expectations, abilities, and individual coping mechanisms (including addictions) into the relationship. We must take responsibility for that.

Many of us have discovered that we have expected our partners to solve our family-of-origin issues or other individual issues. We are often angry at our partners because they don't resolve feelings that belong to us

III

individually. Unless our individual recoveries are strong and we can take ownership of our "baggage," couple recovery will be difficult. In many ways, couple 12-Step work depends on individual 12-Step work.

This theme requires a strong commitment to the 12-Step process. We strongly suggest that both members of a relationship be in an individual 12-Step program. At the bare minimum, both members should believe in the 12-Step process and be willing to learn more about it as individuals and as a couple. We recognize that there are times when the pain of a relationship is so great that it needs the immediate support of our fellowship, even if one partner is new to recovery (or both are).

Founder's Address

Pat C.

First RCA Convention

Minneapolis, Minnesota

August 9, 1991

Look at you! It is amazing to see you all here. I am moved and honored and very blessed to be in your presence. It is hard not to fast forward to the importance and the significance of all of you coming from across the country to be together. Someday, we may all be sitting across the swimming pool saying: "Remember that first RCA weekend? 47 couples attended!"

I can recount in my life that there were times when I got involved in things, and I really didn't know where they were going to end up. I feel that this is true about this moment.

I would like to start with my history and what I think the significance is for me personally.

It starts with a story with which I think many of you will identify, because the common denominator of codependency and addiction is abandonment and feeling the isolation and loneliness on which addictive and codependent obsession thrive.

I have been thinking a lot about my life as a kid. I grew up on a farm. My nearest friend was about a half mile away. In addition to the compulsive working, my Dad's drinking and all the other things going on in our house, I was left alone a lot. My Dad was a professional animal trainer, and we had animals. I found that my friends and the beings in my life that I looked to for comfort were the surrounding animals. Throughout much of my life, one of the things I have searched for has been community. I have gravitated toward things and those organizations that could provide me with a sense of community.

I remember that as a graduate student I was so frightened of being with people. I wondered if I would be accepted. The grad students had coffee breaks in the morning, and I would anguish about attending because my hand would shake when I would hold that cup of coffee. Of course, the more I would try to control it, the more my hand would shake.

I would always be embarrassed that I might spill the coffee. That little terror I had experienced in much of my life and I wanted to feel accepted in the community. This was in the early '70's. I did not know about Adult Children of Alcoholics, and I did not know about many of the things that

1

now we take for granted. At that time professionally, one of the things I was attracted to was the notion of family therapy. We did know that people progressed more with family and marital counseling approaches than by doing things individually. In fact, there was already research in the early '70's about the fact that it was unethical to try to treat people individually for problems that were of a family and marital nature. Often people got worse with individual treatment. So, the ethical thing was to use family and marriage approaches; but I looked around me, and there were not many people doing that kind of counseling.

In 1976 I was asked to start a treatment center. When the hospital asked me how that treatment should be configured, I said that it should be family-centered; in other words, we should have whole families come in. At that time, that was pretty unusual thinking. We started a ten-week program where whole families would come in. The kids would be there starting at about age 6. We started out with chemically addicted families, and eventually we extended treatment to sexually addicted and incest families and used the same formula. These people who came for treatment with their spouses and children had individual and peer group meetings in the afternoon and family group in the evening. Afterwards at about 9:30 or 10:00 p.m., five or six of these families would head down to the pie shop and buy themselves a couple of pies and go over to someone's house and do group all over again until about 2 a.m. Then they would go to work the next day, and they would come into the treatment program at 3 o'clock in the afternoon saying: "Boy, treatment wears you out!"

The problem they were having was that they just didn't go to bed! It took me awhile to figure out what was going on. Then I realized that they were just so hungry to be a part of a group. They had wanted to be part of a group, an extended family, where they were with older people and younger people who were bonded as families. They felt that this was the way it was supposed to be, and somehow they had missed this in life. The reason they didn't want to go home was because it felt so good to be together. Never before had they belonged to a group of people like this. As I watched those families, one of the things that impressed me was that there was a sense of community. Many of those people are still close and connected with one another to this day.

As I reflect on this, I think that we live in a culture that is almost antithetical to community. When we note the history of how people lived together in earlier times, it was a community of people who raised a community of children. This is the first time in history that we have asked just two people to raise children. If you were in a community of people raising a community of children and you saw a child doing something wrong, then you felt partially responsible to stop that kid, to set some limits, or do something appropriate. Now, when we see someone else's kid doing something wrong or hazardous, we say: "Someone should do something about that." We don't feel like we have a right to intervene, because we don't have the connection to do that. The point is that in earlier times, there was a sense of connect-edness.

Now, that is not to say that in earlier times there was an ideal family life. Until the last century, there were large parts of this world in which the father of the family had the right to terminate a child's life. We have made extraordinary progress in terms of our ability to visualize how childhood can be very different. The point I am making is that there was a sense of community, and while we have made progress in some ways, we have really stepped backwards in other ways. The people we really feel sorry for in this day and time are single parents who are raising kids by themselves. The reality is that there may be some couples sitting here that are sweating it out alone raising kids where there are just two parents involved. Indeed, the aunts and uncles, the other people and all the varied parts of the community that were usually involved in a child's life are missing today. We could spend a whole evening just pointing to the ways that we seem to be dismantled and disconnected from one another.

The next important event in my life was my exposure to a base community. Base communities were started by the Catholic Church in Central America because of the shortage of priests. In base communities, family units would commit to one another liturgically, emotionally, and in social action. Six or seven families would become very involved in each others' lives as a community. There was a time in the late '70's (and at that time I was married), when we got involved in a base community. There were six other families in our base community.

In some ways these were the three best years of my life. For three years, we did things together. There was this incredible feeling that you had other adults to talk to, people who witnessed your life. I could get involved with their kids, and they could get involved with my kids. It took the pressure off being a parent in some ways. It took the pressure off being a partner in some ways. In other words, there could be women and men friends in that group, and we could have that intimacy.

That experience had a very profound impact on me, because I knew I wanted that in my life.

In some ways, this was part of the genesis of thinking about the "We Came To Believe" program. I know, conceptually, that when people struggle with relationships that, in fact, relationships have a life of their own. A relationship is more than the individuals who make it up.

One of the things that we used to do at that first treatment center (mentioned earlier) was an exercise conducted which we would do about every ten weeks. One of the assignments was given to people as they came in the door. We would have the children there; we would have the adults there, both single folks and partnered folks. We would ask the kids to pick out new brothers and sisters. Then they would have to pick out new parents. And then as a new family, they would have to go out and spend the evening together and do something none of them had ever done before.

3

Now, it had a little risk to it! You could have a woman in the group who hadn't talked to another man in 17 years, and suddenly she's got another woman's husband, for example. What you did, you see, is to change the rules on them.

Initially when those families would first come into treatment, referral sources would say: "These are all the things that are wrong with the family: They don't know how to send 'I messages'; they don't know how to listen; they don't know how to differentiate; they don't know how to problem solve; they don't know how to resolve conflict; they don't know how to deal with anger; they don't know how to set boundaries; the list is endless. They don't know how to have fun; they don't know how to do things."

But the amazing thing is that when you put them with other people's kids and other people's partners, they knew how to be respectful and how to observe boundaries. They knew how to send "I messages" and listen and have fun. They could be themselves and enjoy one another! And they had a great time.

And they'd come back at the end of the evening and always, inevitably, somebody would get reflective and say: "Why is it that I can be this way with the people I don't live with? And then, with people whom I care about the most, I can't be that way?"

See, it isn't that they didn't know how to do those things. What they were experiencing was clearly their illness. In other words, the pathology in their relationship had a life of its own. I know this is one of the things that happens to all of us, because we have the inheritance that we bring with us from our family-of-origin. We also have whatever we have created between us. Those systems are very strong.

What really has happened is that we have seen an extraordinary amount of progress in what we can do individually with people. But we have not taken our knowledge and instituted it in a way that a couple could take those Twelve Steps. If you were a family therapist who was starting from scratch and trying to figure out an ideal way for a couple to deal with those central dilemmas which every couple faces, you could not devise a better system than the Twelve Steps. But no one ever, ever, developed that system for couples to do.

So, the other part of our work that was important to me was the "Don't Call It Love" survey, which involved a thousand people, some of whom are here tonight. We interviewed them as couples and as individuals. When we really started looking at the data, one of the things that became very clear was that the people who made it the furthest, who were doing the best, who were feeling great about themselves and feeling the most whole, were those people who had support for their coupleship!

In other words, there are lots of people who had support individually, but they didn't have support for their relationship. Let's use Mark's example from his talks about couples' fighting:

"I get my army and my supporters in my group, and you get your army and your supporters in your group." Couples didn't have the witnessing of supporters who had the whole picture, and couples did not get support from people with the complete perspective. As we observed this, it partially prompted us to start the "We Came To Believe" weekends.

Now, it seems to me, that there is basically only one problem that couples have, and I would like to talk a little about it. The ideas may sound very simplistic, but actually this is the truth: The basic thing that all couples have to deal with is, "How to be separate and individual, and how to be paired, at the same time? How do you do those two things simultaneously?"

I would like to stop for a moment and just reflect a little bit about what the dilemma means for us as recovering people. Let's talk about: What does that mean in terms of our own individual pieces? In terms of the pieces we bring that are ours? The part about being separate and the part about being ourselves? I think that there are lots of resources available to us. And, also what is the inner life of ourselves that we need to listen to?

I believe that spirituality is truly being able to look around in your life and notice the metaphors. To be able to seek (out of those metaphors, those analogies, those things where we are constantly listening to what's going on) and to say: "How is that like my life? What is the message in that for me?" Because the messages are all around us if we listen to them.

I had a dream earlier this year which I think illustrated that for me. Some of you know this part of my story. One of the struggles in my life is that my father is an alcoholic who was sober for 35 years and started drinking about four years ago. And about 18 months ago, it really plunged me into a whole new round of therapy. And here I am. I'm 46 years old. I've been in this field; I've been in recovery for 14 years; I've got to waste my time going to therapy; and there I was. It's been a very powerful year for me in terms of some of the things I did not know that I now have learned. It's like there are big pieces of a puzzle that have just come to me.

The dream that I had was very helpful to me because the dream was about two hawks. There was a snowstorm. As the hawks were flying by me, I could see that the male hawk had been injured somehow. He was flying and he was keeping up. There was a female hawk and a male hawk and the male hawk was keeping up, but I could see that it was a struggle. So I grabbed them out of the air, both of them. I expected that the injured hawk was going to struggle and try to get away. I was surprised because the hawk knew that I was trying to help and heal him. As I pulled him close to me, he nestled next to me and was loving me in response. I was moved by that. As I was walking back to the house, I stumbled, and I dropped the hawk. And I thought, "That blew it, because for sure he'll fly away." But he waited for me, and I picked him up. He nestled against me again, and I brought him inside. The tip of his wing had been broken, and the children and I set his wing.

5

As I told that story to my therapist, we both ended up crying. In many ways the dream was a metaphor about how therapy has been for me, in that I've worked very hard at it. I felt the good will of my child, that there was a part of me that was willing to be healed and to stay there while the adult part of me took care of me. It was a very powerful thing for me to listen for, because I think that is the suffering that all of us deal with in our individual recoveries. It is the gift you bring to your partner. And it is that willingness and the suffering, I think, which are some of the gifts of recovery.

You know, I've been really struck by commercials that sort of make fun of 12-Step meetings, where people get up and say I'm a such-and-such-aholic and what have you. In some ways, at first, I kind of cringe when I hear it, because for me, they are mocking something sacred. Yet, on the other hand, there is also the fact that the recovery movement is impacting this culture and others are having to deal with it. And while it is appearing in commercials, something has made a difference.

The other thing that I think we bring to a coupleship as part of our individual recoveries is that we learned how to "de-people" the room. Whenever you come to a relationship, you bring all of those interactions that you had with others in your formative years. The critical issue is: to become clear about "what is about your family-of-origin" as opposed to "what is about yourselves."

I know, for me, that dream has involved some really intense struggles in this past year. One of the gifts in my life is a man named Louie Anderson. You may have read some of Louie's stuff. One of the things in his book is videotaping his family. I thought, "What a great idea." So I found my videotape camera, and I told my folks that I wanted them to have a talk about their childhoods and their growing up and their marriage and what-have-you. It was a very powerful experience for me.

I'm the second child in my family. I have an older sister who was born dead. It was in 1941, on All Saints' Day that she was born dead. My uncle was a physician, and his partner delivered the baby. My uncle swooped in and grabbed the baby. My mother never saw. As she told the story, in those days there were no grief groups. There wasn't anybody to talk to; there was no debriefing for her. And she was in the Red Cross and as you remember, December 7th wasn't far behind. So when she got out of the hospital, she immediately was immersed in all the activities of the Red Cross, in the early days of World War II. The fact was that the first time she ever talked about it since 1941 was on that tape.

I was real struck by it, because for myself, I was aware of her tremendous sadness. And then, I realized, that played a part in my own addiction, my own recovery. One of the things I've had to learn is about my interaction patterns. How, in my life, I have sought out very sad women. I learned how my life might have been very different. Picture with me now--I was the second kid. My father was away at war. My mother lost her first child, so when I came, I became a special child for her: one that took up a lot of her

6

energy and her focus and her sadness. The result for me was that it set up a series of dynamics of which I didn't really have a clear picture. What I learned is that I had carried these dynamics into my marriages.

I think that part of your activities as members of RCA (and that one of the things which you bring with you from your individual recovery to your relationship) is that you have to take care of your individual business. We all have stories about the families we come from, and the ways that we impose those things, or find matches in our relationships.

The second task you have to deal with is bonding. How do you connect and make commitments to people? I myself am now having to deal with the issues of dating, which is interesting in my family. For openers, just explaining to people what I do, is interesting. In my dating, there are complications when I have felt it important to talk about my recovery as a sex addict. There is never a really graceful way.

I remember one occasion and a woman who was a very dear friend. We started dating, and the level of connection was such that I thought it important for her to start knowing a little bit about me. So I said: "You know, it would be really important to me that you read this book, "Out Of The Shadows." So she read the book. And when she finished the book, I said: "I have some things to tell you," and I did [tell her]. It was about a month later that I'd read a great novel called, "The Wolf's Hour," which is a novel about werewolves. I said: "You know, you really ought to read this book." She gave the book back to me and she said it was a good book. I don't know where this came from in me, but there is this impish side of me, and I said: "There's one other thing I need to tell you about me!" And just for a moment, I could see it had crossed her mind. One of the things I got out of that relationship is that I think that she is one of the people with whom I learned what it's like to be me in a relationship.

I feel presumptuous in front of you folks. I mean, we joke about my being the honorary single member of RCA; but you guys are the people who have labored the good fight and are here now. You are doing it. So it is sort of presumptuous of me talking about having relationships. But the part that I've learned out of my dating experience (which has got to be the same as yours), is that the criterion for success of the relationship is when I can be with you and feel most myself. The degree that those pieces aren't there is the degree of my discomfort.

One of the things that I have seen RCA couples do, and which I think is an astounding and wonderful gift, is couples exchange pictures of each other as children. So you always have in front of you a sense of the vulnerability of your partner, and that there is this child within you to whom you also need to attend. I think that part of bonding (like my hawk dream) is that we can attend to each others' vulnerability and build our trust that adults can in fact be trustworthy.

I believe also that the toughest part for those of us who come out of shame-based systems, is that righteousness can be in our way and lead us down a path in which we can be very blind. I am sure that there are such times in your families (this has happened to everybody in here, I know). There has been a time when you are absolutely certain something was such, and you swore it was, and everybody in the family said: "No, you don't know what this is like." And you said: "Absolutely not," and you knew it. Only [later] it became clear with incontrovertible evidence that you were wrong. I hate that thought. And, I learned one of the things that can be most deadly for me is righteousness, especially if that righteousness is connected with my anger.

Not long ago, I was really upset and angry and in a very righteous place. I stomped into my bedroom, and I flipped on the TV. There were the Ninja Turtles, the Teenage Mutant Ninja Turtles! For those of you who don't know the story, there is a character in that show (it's a great story) called Splinter, who is kind of an overgrown rat and who is also like a zen monk. He says these very wise things. He is the one who has raised these four Mutant Ninja Turtles and taught them their martial arts and given them their wisdom. Splinter's words came right out of the TV and said: (he was talking to Raphael) "You know, Raphael, your anger will destroy you." I backed up and I sat down, and I listened to Splinter's two-minute dialogue with Raphael about how his anger was going to eat him from within and destroy him. It was the best thing I've heard in a long time. I had a friend who said: "That story would be truly great if the TV would have gone on by itself!"

The point is: all of us need to be aware (because of the nature of how shame works) that one of the greatest impediments to bonding is the fact of our righteousness and our anger. This is not about holding onto our truths and standing for our boundaries and all those things, but I'm talking about that blaming dynamic, that feeling where my happiness is somehow impaired because the other person isn't doing something right. My experience both in watching people recover and in my whole life and as a family and marital therapist is this one [people think,] "I need that approval." And after you have seen that one hundredth couple in therapy, it just seems incongruent. We do our own happiness make!

So the value, I think, of what you guys are doing is that you are really creating a revolution in the 12-Step communities! The 12 Steps are a very disciplined way to live your life as a couple. We are in a stage in our history where we are going through a traumatic revolution. We are seeing it in terms of watching the democracies across the world. None of us two years ago could have forecast what is happening in terms of democracy. What we don't realize is that there are other kinds of revolutions that are happening. It was at the same time that the Magna Carta was written in 1215 that across Europe whole movements around courtship [were also happening]. And the notion which was new in Western Civilization and new on the planet was that you got to choose your partner. Joseph Campbell talks about that as being one of the most extraordinary revolutions in mankind's history. And, in fact, just to give you perspective on this, last fall an article came out about studies of couples in China. China is an incredibly interesting place for family study. Couples who had their marriages arranged (which is how it has been for lots of people on the planet) were compared with couples who chose their partners. The couples who chose their partners were dramatically happier, especially the women, than the people who had their marriages and partnerships arranged.

Now, the important thing about that, you see, is: I believe that a relationship is a continuum of choice. Every day it brings a choice. And it is in the wrinkling of that choice, you see, that a lot of people get stuck. This is because the relationship becomes sort of a given. "This is what I have got to do," as opposed to recognizing that "This is my choice." Every relationship has its suffering. I like Scott Peck's phrase. He says: "Every relationship is an ordeal. The question is how to make it the best ordeal you can find." The reality is that this is a tough challenge.

What you are about and the significance in all this is that the recovery movement has really started a new culture and whole new ways of being. People have popularized principles that have been learned in therapy. People are interacting on different levels now than they were twenty years ago. I listen to my children. The thought that I could have had the psychological awareness at sixteen that they do, drives me nuts! My sixteen year old daughter looked at me and said: "You know, your parenting has become counterproductive." She says: "Your consequence is going to make me more defiant, and I am going to act out more, and it's going to be your fault." This is the same child with whom I failed to connect during a trip I had taken. When I travel, I usually connect with my kids daily, and for three or four days I had not connected. It had been a particularly hectic trip and for a number of reasons we had not hooked up. When I came back, she looked at me and said: "Dad, when you live between two houses, you don't have a geographical place which is your center. So, people are my center. When I don't hear from you, I lose my center." You see all you can say to a kid who says something like that is: "I can't wait to see your children!"

The recovery work we are doing is bringing these notions of different ways of relating. The fact is that we in recovery are twenty million strong in this country. You can't have ten percent of this population doing what we do, and not have the ripple effect on the rest of the population. We will never raise children the same again, because of what 12-Step communities are doing.

And you know, people criticize. We have our critics, usually academics, and forgive me, but sometimes they also come out of their own pathology. In their criticisms, one of the things they really have to deal with is the fact that people are doing [12-Step programs] because it is renewal to them and because it makes a difference and because their lives are better. And so, what's happening is that the recovery movement is becoming popularized. I look at John Bradshaw, for example. *Homecoming* is a book. People in New

York are still trying to figure out what has happened, because that book sold 610,000 copies in three months. No non-fiction book in the history of this planet has ever done that! Novels, perhaps, but no non-fiction book has ever done that. Which says there is a need there.

People in the academic community and the critical community can't figure out what this means. The fact is when we start dealing with those vulnerable, inner-child feelings within ourselves, transformations occur. It's the recovery movement that's helping us get better. It is the recovery movement which says, "You know, I've produced a lot of suffering." The healing starts! We are becoming more responsible for our own healing. No longer is there going to be just physicians telling us what to do. In fact, one of the things that's happening is that the biggest watchers of continuing medical education is, guess what? It's not physicians. On Sunday mornings, there are programs designed to teach doctors about what this illness is. There are only about 63,000 physicians who watch those programs. Six million other people watch them! Six million people and they have a common characteristic. They have a chronic disease of some kind, of which one of the leading ones is alcoholism.

What you have is more and more people taking responsibility for their healing. So physicians are having to deal with the fact that some of their patients know more about their illness than they do. And God knows in sex addiction, that is the truth. Many times addicts and codependents have had to teach their therapists about themselves and their illnesses. We are making a difference and that suffering can be a badge of courage.

I also believe that it is the 12-Step communities which are bringing spirituality back to this country and that people are living in the spirit. And I believe that there's a rift between those forces which have destroyed it and how the 12-Step communities have grown. I do believe that there is stuff that is emanating. What this is about, and what I'm now saying is that you as a recovering couple sort of have that extra added quality, and that you are adding another message. Historically, a characteristic, and (now I'm going back to AA) one of the things that people coming out of shame-based, codependent, addictive families have ended up doing, is viewing things in very black and white ways. They become rigid about it. So they take recovery and make it rigid. In other words they "sacredize" the 12 Steps, and make it so they can never change anything. And, you see, the 12 Steps need to change. If you went to a meeting for everything for which you qualified, you would not have a life left! This [RCA] is the one group that you can come to with whatever things you've got! And during the meeting, it's OK. This is the one place you can do that.

The second thing is that you are putting a value on coupleship after a time when we have been extraordinarily mindful about the individual, the new generation, and the culture of narcissism. You are coming to a time where you are giving the message about the value of bonding, and that it is a good thing to be in a bonded relationship. There is a value to that.

10

I have some hopes for you. This is the second time that I have been present when a fellowship got started in my lifetime. I remember the early days of SAA. I remember how frightened we were, and how we had this men's spirituality group. We didn't want the church to know quite what it was that we were doing. Out of the first ten members of SAA, nine of them were therapists, and God knows we didn't want our clients to know! So we started another group that was the Wednesday night group. However, what happened was that in the first two or three years we grew very slowly because of fear. We always had this logic that we have to figure out what we are doing before we tell anybody else (which I think was perfectionism on our part). I think what we needed to do was let many people in the door, and let them start talking from where the problems were. I believe that this board has done that in the spirit of inviting you in, and investing you with the responsibility to help articulate what needs to happen now. One of the things I hope that you are willing to do (because you truly are different from the other fellowships) is perhaps to write a group conscience of what's said. All of us are new in this program. My plea to you is that you be open to doing that.

The second thing is to recognize that we are as imperfect as we are. This organization will have its imperfections, just like in our relationships we have imperfections. We need to be tolerant and to allow things to unfold. You know, sometimes things take an incredible amount of time.

I had an experience earlier this year that was very moving for me. I had been involved with a woman twenty years ago, and I lived with her for about a year. It was a very devastating experience for me. Some of you have heard my monologue on the "velcro woman."

Basically, that was this relationship. She clearly was also a sex addict. One of the things that happened for me was that I got a phone call from her this past year, and she asked me out to lunch. Her story was that she is now recovering, and her therapist had assigned her the task of going out and getting a 12-Step workbook. She couldn't find the one that she had been assigned, but she ran across *The Gentle Path*. For her, it was two days of a great deal of pain. And she said: "You were even thinking about those things back then, and I was in such a funk that I had no idea what you were trying to say, and I'm sorry." She spent the rest of that lunch making amends for all the things that happened. And, I found myself saying that this is what making amends is. It allowed me then to make amends for all the hurts that I caused. I found my inner self just making a gigantic shift with that healing. And what I realized was that it took twenty years for that to happen! Twenty years!

When we think of the program, we think that it should happen in one year or it should happen in two years and what-have-you. For some of these things to come together, there is God's timing. I find myself very impatient and wanting all these things to happen at once. I believe that the timing for this particular experience in my life was absolutely perfect. It gave me

11

some things which were very, very helpful, and the timing was perfect. From the perspective of this organization, you need not look at the timeline as one year or two years, but you need to think of decades of time.

I truly hope that what happens this weekend is that RCA becomes a non-Minneapolis based organization. These people here have labored very hard. It is a lot of work. I don't know how you guys are going to work things out, but my hope is that the representation on the board will fully reflect a nationwide perspective. You may still have a Minneapolis post office box and central office and keep all the mechanics of that here. The point is that the board, however, needs to reflect a national perspective. So, if you are sitting there, and you are saying that it sounds like something you could do, but you live in Fresno or wherever, remember the RCA board needs to have you folks as part of it.

My other hope for you is that you do not hide your recovery. I have traveled around this country, and there are a lot of you who are not here tonight. I have met RCA groups all over, and I know there are places where I have met people and those people are not here. My hope is that you continue your outreach, that those folks will get an opportunity to come, and we really do let the world know what RCA is all about.

I hope you have a good time. I know a lot of you, and so I trust that this weekend will be a lot of fun for you.

I hope this group makes some effort to reach out to minorities and oppressed people. I was recently talking with an RCA couple in North Carolina who have an amazing story. One of their recovery issues (and this man is a sex addict) is that his son announced to him that he was gay, and that he had a lover and that he wanted his parents to accept him. The mother was moved by the integrity of the son saying that this was the truth and that he wanted his lover to be accepted by his parents. She welcomed this young man. This was not true of the father. He was troubled. It was his RCA community that told him to "lighten up." Today he cherishes this young man, and it was one of the real milestones in their RCA recovery. I was moved by the lesbian couple seated at the back. My invitation is that we not blind ourselves again to the needs of oppressed and misunderstood individuals.

It may seem like a simple thing to put one of these conferences together, to agonize over trying to maintain your recovery, but also going to meetings and board meetings to get things done. It is a lot of work, you guys. These are true troopers up here in this front row. I want to take a moment and recognize their contribution. I watched you. I know what you did. You deserve the credit. You've done well.

It has been a pattern in my life to start things that I guess I needed myself. And here I am once again. I have a final wish for myself. You see, I know what you guys have got, and I know what the potential is for you, and my wish is that someday I'll be able to join you.
Thanks.

12

A GUIDE TO RCA's TWELVE STEPS

Step 1

We admitted we were powerless over our relationship - that our lives together had become unmanageable.

We all have family-of-origin issues and a history of relationships. We may not have gotten what we needed emotionally, physically, mentally or spiritually when we were growing up. There may have been abuse (physical, sexual, spiritual, emotional), abandonment, or deprivation. We all bring "baggage" to the coupleship. The steps teach us how to look at our baggage and how to reverse the process of blame.

Both of us are responsible for the presence or absence of intimacy between us. As soon as each of us accepts mutual responsibility, we are ready for the First Step of RCA. Step One involves taking 200% responsibility for the health or disease of the relationship. Each person carries 100%.

Occasionally a couple may not have been far enough along in their individual recoveries to be able to answer the following questions, or they may have gotten into a fight or into dysfunction simply by having issues raised. If this were the case, we encouraged step work be done only in the presence of a sponsoring couple.

We also recognized that some couples came to our meetings having met after both partners had been in individual recovery for various periods of time. They may not have had a long history of coupleship dysfunction or other dysfunction. In those cases, Step One involved understanding old dysfunctional patterns with other partners. It also involved understanding family-of-origin issues, personality traits and other individual issues that might have affected the relationship.

Writing is very important. It is suggested that the couple take one pencil and one piece of paper and begin the process together. RCA is about the "we"-ness and "us"-ness of our relationship. In Recovering Couples Anonymous, we open ourselves up to a new way of thinking and living in coupleship.

Now that you have that piece of paper, make a couple decision. Who will hold the pencil and do the writing? Are you able to share, negotiate or compromise? Is there a power struggle? Are you ready to take the First Step? Now read aloud the "Safety Guidelines."

Divide the paper in half with a line down the middle. Make a list. You are now ready to answer the following questions:

• *What dysfunctional roles had we brought from our families-of-origin?*

• *What had our family-of-origin model taught us about relationships?*

13

• *What were our individual experiences of abuse and how had those affected our ability to be related, to be intimate, and to be sexual?*

• *How had our individual addictions affected our relationship?*

• *What were the unmanageable issues we never seemed to resolve? (e.g., how we spend money, how we spend our time together, parenting the kids, dividing the household duties, where/how we celebrated holidays, etc.)*

• *How had these issues brought us to anger and what were our patterns of expressing anger?*

• *How had we felt hopeless about our relationship?*

• *In order to save our relationship, what measures had we tried that hadn't seemed to work?*

• *How had we fought unfairly?*

Having surrendered thus far, we were ready to take Step Two.

Step 2

We came to believe that a power greater than ourselves could restore us to commitment and intimacy.

In Step One we admitted we were powerless over our relationship. Step Two involves coming to some mutual understanding of what we trusted as a couple and what we believed in as a couple.

We sought to blend our heritage and to find something to believe as a couple. We made a collage of this belief to have a visual picture of our "greater power." We found this helpful to frame and keep accessible to our relationship and to share with other couples. We were willing to accept a Higher Power and nurture our relationship with a sense of hope and freedom.

We also found more intimacy in sharing with each other our Second Steps from our individual programs. We may have come from different religious backgrounds or no religious background at all. Writing the step remains a useful tool in relationships. We suggest you share one pencil and piece of paper as you do the steps. These are a list of questions to consider as you discover the spiritual path of recovery for yourselves.

Pause and read aloud the Safety Guidelines before moving forward.

- *What family-of-origin messages about religion or spirituality had we brought into the relationship?*

- *What kinds of instruction, modeling, teaching, etc. about religion or spirituality had we experienced?*

- *Did we receive any guidance from our parents?*

- *What abuses and/or dysfunctional beliefs about couples did we learn from our religion? What healthy and supportive beliefs did we learn from our church, synagogue or other house of worship?*

- *Had we experienced any spiritual abuse? (Were one of our parents the higher power in your family-of-origin? Were clergy, religions teachers or nuns unkind, shaming, blaming or belittling?)*

- *Had we felt angry about religion, God, or our heritage?*

- *Had we trusted and accepted or mistrusted and rejected the religious traditions of our partner?*

- *What had been our spiritual history as a couple?*

Step 3

We made a decision to turn our wills and our life together over to the care of God as we understood God.

Together two people who are in a committed relationship form a coupleship, a oneness, a distinct and separate entity. This coupleship has a life of its own and needs to be nurtured appropriately. Couple recovery depends on this nurturance. Both partners need individual recovery: meetings, sponsors, therapy, a support group, spirituality, recreation, vocation and other individual interests. A coupleship needs these same elements for couple recovery.

Trust is said to be a major issue for couples, as their experience of trust was violated in previous relationships/family-of-origin.

Step Three involved what we decided to trust together and how we decided to turn our relationship over to a "Higher Power."

Before Step Three could be completed, we went on a "spiritual quest." Bring out your piece of paper and begin a "list" again. On all of your steps, "date" your papers so in referring to them you are able to monitor your growth in this program. "Spiritual quests" vary widely and can involve things such as:

- *start each day with thanksgiving to our Higher Power*
- *reading scripture together*
- *doing daily meditations*
- *going to church or other house of worship*
- *going to study groups*
- *praying together*
- *a daily walk to enjoy nature*
- *making a trip or a retreat to a spiritually significant place*

These quests could have taken days, months or years before a mutually acceptable "statement of faith" would occur. We were encouraged to write down a quest agreement. It could be in longhand, or typed suitable for framing and witnessed by "couple" friends or a "sponsoring couple." This presents a truly warm, supportive and validating experience for all people involved. It is suggested the couple chair a "step meeting" in RCA and share their experience, strength and hope with other couples.

Ultimately, Step Three involved turning our relationship over.

Many couples found it significant to do something formal, traditional (even sacramental) or non-traditional. An example of this was a re-dedication of vows in the presence of friends or even someone of spiritual authority. Some people have re-dedicated their coupleship in a church or synagogue. Some have gone to a bed and breakfast, some have had a picnic with friends in the park, or invited guests to their home for a celebration of their spiritual renewal.

We are invited to be a creative couple and have a memorable event celebrating our increasing commitment to ourselves, each other, and the relationship.

Recognize that we are both on a spiritual path together. Placing our relationship in our Higher Power's hands would mean the end of power struggles and control. We made a decision. We have surrendered. And this is the basic spiritual principle upon which Step Three stands.

Step 4

*We made a searching and fearless moral inventory
of our relationship together as a couple.*

Each partner needs first to look at the impact of their behavior on the relationship. After having shared the individual inventories with each other, the inventory of the coupleship is completed. The goal of this inventory is to gain awareness about the extent of the damage has the illness caused. We must fearlessly face our coupleship. When a couple is able to face the reality of their relationship, they can grow in their love based on honesty.

Review these questions about your personal role in the relationship:

- **Unfinished Business:** In what ways have I not finished things with my partner, letting them go and fester?

- **Hypervigilance:** In what ways have I looked for things to go wrong?

- **Self-Responsibility:** In what ways have I failed to take responsibility for my mistakes or issues?

- **Comfort and Feelings:** In what ways have I not shared uncomfortable feelings with my partner?

- **Accuracy and Honesty:** In what ways have I placated my partner or opposed sharing real perceptions?

- **Connection:** In what ways have I not been available to my partner? Do I seek regular ways to connect?

- **Stress:** In what ways do my overextension and stress affect my partner?

- **Separateness:** Do I develop a separate life away from my partner? Does this separate life include friends and activities?

- **Personal Needs:** In what ways is my partner to guess or "know" about my needs? Do I ask for them to be met clearly?

- **Shame Avoidance:** In what ways do I seek to put blame on my partner?

- **Pain Thresholds:** In what ways have I tolerated pain that was unnecessary?

- **Choice Clarity:** In what ways have I been unclear about my choices, leaving things undecided or up to my partner?

To complete the inventory, review together these questions and record your answers on a single piece of paper. Writing helped us organize our thoughts. Begin by reading aloud the Safety Guidelines.

Answer the following questions as a couple:

- *In what ways have we created crisis when there wasn't any?*

17

- *In what ways have we had fights which really never accomplished anything?*

- *How have we neglected instead of nurtured our relationship?*

- *How do we avoid being close when we have the opportunity to have intimacy?*

- *In what ways do we pretend these problems do not exist?*

- *In what ways have we isolated ourselves from other couples and friends who could support our relationship?*

- *In what ways have we been depleted both physically and emotionally so we had nothing to give one another?*

- *In what ways have we tolerated abuse of ourselves and our family?*

- *What are our social and physical strengths?*

- *How had the disease of our relationship affected us socially, financially, and physically?*

- *What had we grieved together as a couple? How did we grieve?*

- *What did our process look like?*

- *What were our losses, (e.g. having never achieved our financial goals, having children with problems, having a dysfunctional sexual relationship, etc.)?*

- *Despite our dysfunctions, what had we liked about our relationship?*

- *What had been the good things?*

- *What had we treasured in each other and the coupleship?*

You are now ready for Step Five.

Step 5

We admitted to God, to each other and to
another couple the exact nature of our wrongs.

Most of us chose to share our Fourth Step with a Sponsoring Couple or some other couple who had been in the program long enough to have worked most of the Twelve Steps. It was also important to give this inventory to a couple who were, in our opinion, living the program.

This process of doing the Fifth Step was a vehicle to self-acceptance in our coupleship. This may have been difficult because some aspects and behavior of the relationship were shameful. This was our opportunity to have our guilt and shame transformed into humility.

Call your Sponsoring Couple on the telephone and schedule an evening to share your inventory. Allow about two hours in length. Choose a safe place. Get a good night's sleep. Consume your evening meal before meeting. Do not be rushed or committed to anything else that evening/time. Get comfortable--have tea, juice or coffee available. The Sponsoring Couple has a piece of paper and pencil handy to make notes for later input. Allow the couple to share at their own pace--and keep focused. As part of this process, the Sponsoring Couple has the opportunity to practice active listening.

Start with a moment of silence and then the Serenity Prayer. Follow by reading the Safety Guidelines aloud.

We found that sharing honestly and openly with another couple was healing for both the grief and shame. We realized the coupleship was accepted, validated and appreciated in spite of the dysfunctional behaviors.

We encourage couples to record their experience in a journal. We also find it helpful for the Sponsoring Couple to provide a written impression of the Sponsored Couple's 5th Step. Feedback can be given either in the journal, in the Big Book, or in a note or a card of encouragement.

This step freed us to begin anew.

Step 6

We were entirely ready to have God remove all these defects of char-
acter, communication and caring.

Step 6 has a clear message--get ready for some changes!

This step emphasizes relationship building and improvement. Relationship building involved recognizing the wrongs, professing them and becoming willing to get rid of them.

Every recovering couple has a series of patterns in which they can lose their reality. These patterns usually occur at times of high stress or periods of overextension or depletion. Sometimes these dysfunctional patterns occur when there is an opportunity for intimacy. One or both partners elect to avoid closeness by going to the old patterns. Recovering couples need to recognize the patterns and the temporary insanity these patterns bring and how a couple can lose their reality together.

Here are some clues for thinking about your loss of reality--or--how do we know when we are crazy?

- *Repetitive arguments*
- *Frequent periods of denial*
- *Nonproductive communications*
- *Extreme overextension or depletion*
- *Making statements you do not mean*
- *Taking actions you regret*
- *Fighting about issues that are not important*

Make these lists together and pick a time to talk when you are both feeling balanced. You are now ready. Enjoy the process. See the humor. Open up to healing in your relationship.

Always start by reading the Safety Guidelines aloud.

Take your piece of paper to make lists and gather more information for your coupleship by answering the following questions:

- *What had been our dysfunctional patterns of relating?*

- *What had been our dysfunctional patterns of communicating?*

- *What had been our dysfunctional patterns of caring?*

- *What had been our dysfunctional patterns of nurturing each other?*

- *What had been our dysfunctional patterns of being sexual?*

- *How had we fought unfairly?*

If as a couple we don't work on our relationship, the same issues will surface with different partners in the next relationship. This means that we must practice couple recovery with our partner. Our couple issues were the same when we got into this relationship as they were in previous relationships.

Step 7

We humbly asked God to remove our shortcomings.

In Step 7, we need to form a working partnership with a power greater than ourselves.

We seek humility--the ability to face reality. The real change happened as we let go of our false pride and worked in partnership to make contracts to change.

The contracts we made were witnessed and signed by our sponsors. We felt validated in our relationship. We had something to remind us of our hard work in self/coupleship recovery.

As we defined our Higher Power, we asked how our trust in that Power could help us remove those defects of character. Where could we get help to know how to communicate, fight fairly, have a healthy sex life, etc.? RCA believes strongly in making contracts. We needed contracts about:

- **Sexuality:** For example, we may have seen a therapist for insight and direction regarding specific attitudes and behaviors. We may have attempted celibacy contracts to take sexual pressure off our relationship in order to work on other issues. We may have needed contracts about how often, who initiates, etc. What were our sexual boundaries?

- **Producing Income:** What are the dynamics of independence when one partner is financially dependent on another?

- **Division of Labor:** What is the impact on the division of labor in the household when both partners work outside the home? When only one works outside the home? When both are retired?

- **Communicating:** We were encouraged to look at the Safety Guidelines in order to know how to structure a contract about communicating. As partners, we were encouraged to use "I statements" rather than saying "you did..." or "you said..." This helped us each take individual responsibility for the coupleship and helped us avoid blame.

- **Recreation:** How would we play together? We may have been abused out of our playfulness as a couple. We needed to deal with unresolved expectations. Why is having fun such hard work sometimes? A recreation contract was helpful for some couples.

- **Parenting:** Who had certain responsibilities and when? Did we agree on discipline and what values we wished to pass on to our children? Did we stand united in our religious and/or philosophical beliefs? Or did we allow our children to be buffeted between two opposing viewpoints on life? Were

21

we confused about our parenting roles? Did we allow our children to
"divide and conquer?" Or did we maintain unity in parenting?

- **Fighting:** Conflict is healthy but fighting unfairly is not. We took the list
  of how we fought unfairly from Steps One and/or Six, and made another
  list of fighting rules to guide us in conflict in the coupleship. These rules
  varied from couple to couple. For example, if we said, "We always quarrel
  unfairly after 11:00 p.m. We're just too tired," a fighting rule was that
  "We won't conduct a fight after 11:00 p.m." We may agree not to argue
  in the car or in front of the kids, etc. Some general rules that most couples implemented were:

  - In order for a constructive argument to take place, both people
    must agree that there is indeed an issue in conflict and agree on
    an appropriate time and place to discuss this conflict. When agree-
    ment of a time and place is reached, all other "fighting" rules take
    effect.

  - We won't name-call, shame, damage, use offensive language, or
    blame our partners. We will use "I statements" to express our
    needs, feelings and boundaries.

  - We will have a certain time-limit. When time is up we must
    reschedule a time to continue the dispute. We can call "time-out"
    or take "breaks," and we can cancel the fight if rules have been bro-
    ken.

  - For those of us who don't know how to fight or don't like to engage
    in any kind of conflict at all, we will agree to be honest about our
    feelings (including anger), even if this is only for 15 minutes.

  - If we can't fight fairly by ourselves, or if we fear confrontation, we
    will have our verbalizing of disagreements only in the presence of
    our RCA sponsors or our therapist.

  - We agree to avoid dramatic exits and to avoid physical abuse. We
    agree not to threaten divorce. If one of us needs an individual
    time-out to get in touch with feelings, to think about things or to
    feel safe, we can say, "This is not about my leaving the relationship
    or avoiding the conflict issue, but I am taking a break and will be
    back. Do you agree to meet in one hour (or tomorrow morning,
    etc.)? This is not about my abandoning the coupleship."

Again, these were just a few rules. The other rules varied according to the history of each coupleship. They may have seemed oppressive or cumbersome at first. We found that while we needed to be very intentional about them in the first months, they eventually became more automatic as they replaced our old behaviors and became "routine." The goal was to be able to express and hear anger in a healthy way. We experienced the ability to resolve conflict and fight fairly as a great gift of intimacy. Our fighting contracts were written out, each rule elaborated, and witnessed by our RCA sponsors.

Step 8

We made a list of all persons we had harmed and became willing to make amends to them all.

Step 8 is about those people, including ourselves individually, who were harmed by our coupleship dysfunction: family members, children, friends, fellow workers, etc. This step helps us to interact with other people in a new way. This step calls for a change in our behavior. There is a logical sequence for us to follow. First we make a list again--discover how we had harmed ourselves first in the coupleship (i.e., venting rage or holding resentments). What was this harm like? Next, we asked ourselves about our thoughts and feelings about having done that harm. If our relationship has been as crazy as we know it to have been, then there has been harm to others.

Begin to list the "others."

We became willing to make amends by admitting this harm to ourselves and each other and by having changed the nature of our relationship with each other.

It helps to categorize the wrong doings into 3 groups:

Material Wrongs

• *Money--borrowing, spending, withholding*

• *Contracts--cheating, not abiding by terms*

• *Personal Abuse--physical, sexual*

Moral Wrongs

• *Setting bad examples to anyone who looked to you for guidance*

• *Excessive preoccupation or obsessions with people or projects in order to be unavailable to others*

23

•*Sexual infidelity, broken promises, lying, verbal abuse*

Spiritual Wrongs

•*Neglect of obligations to yourself, family, support group, community*

•*Avoiding self-development*

•*Lack of gratitude*

•*Neglect of spiritual quest*

Now we have a better idea about what dysfunctional and diseased behaviors have exsisted in our coupleship.

Now we take a look at the facts and list our fears. What is our resistance to making amends? Are we willing to accept the consequences of our behavior?

How had we intended to make our amends?

In this step, we continue to take our own inventory--as a couple. We check our own progress from time to time.

We reviewed our amends lists with our sponsors. Care was taken to not make amends which would hurt or injure others. When direct amends were not appropriate for couples or individuals we had harmed, we devised to make amends in other ways (i.e., prayed for the well being of these people, etc.)

We discovered that, as we become willing to look at our own behavior, we become more tolerant and forgiving, less rigid and judgmental of other couples. Our viewpoints, attitudes and beliefs are beginning to change as a result of our own participation in this process.

We became ready to move on to Step Nine.

Step 9

We made direct amends to such people wherever possible, except when to do so would injure them or others.

This is another action step and requires that we demonstrate a willingness to confront issues of our past. It takes courage to do this step, a careful sense of timing, and good judgment.

This step has been referred to as having "spiritual surgery" performed on us. Have your Eighth Step list available.

Most RCA couples, for example, begin by doing a Ninth Step with their children. We can make amends to our children by respecting them as individuals, by maintaining our own recovery, and by being healthy and reasonably happy adults ourselves.

Be careful not to confuse apologies with amends. Sometimes apologies are called for, but apologies are not amends. Amends are made by acting differently. For example, we can apologize ten times for being late to the meeting while we are the secretaries, but this will not "amend" the issue. Coming on time and changing our behavior thus becomes our amend.

When we repair the damage we have done to others, we will be "overhauling" our relationship. We will find a glow of satisfaction in knowing we have done everything to pay off every material, moral and spiritual debt we owe our fellow human beings.

When we looked at Step Eight, we realized we had put our own relationship at the top of the list. How do we make amends to ourselves?

First, get a new attitude, one which reflects a willingness to love and forgive ourselves. Think about what we want to say. Be clear. Perhaps we want to write it down and take responsibility for our actions. Both of us must be willing to turn the coupleship over to our Higher Power.

In preparation for the actual making of the amends, we devote time to prayer and meditation. We don't go on if either of us is angry or upset. We keep it simple. We can express a desire or ask permission. "I need to be aware of the harm I have done to others and take responsibility for my actions. I would like to make amends to us/you. Are you OK to receive it?"

Again, create a comfortable, safe setting--kitchen table, living room-- choose the favorite place you like to go. Read the Safety Guidelines and open with a prayer. A sample amends may sound something like this:

"I want to make an amend to our relationship about _____. I forgive myself for all the words that were said out of fear (thoughtlessness, inconsideration, anger, immaturity, selfishness, etc.) and out of my own confusion. I wish no harm to our relationship. I didn't intend to cause you pain. I ask for your forgiveness. I plan to change my behavior by _____."

Step 10

We continued to take personal inventory and when we were wrong promptly admitted it to our partner and to others we had harmed.

The final three steps are about practicing what we have learned in the first nine steps.

Step Ten is about continuing to take inventory of our relationship. We believed that one part of this is what we call the "daily" or "weekly" inventory. The purpose of the daily or weekly inventory is to reverse the process of blaming behaviors that so often haunted many of us. It is also to teach each other what we really liked and what we really appreciate in each other. The hope is to find that this new behavior becomes so familiar and automatic that we can do it without needing to write everything down.

Each partner takes a sheet of paper and divides it in half. On one side of the paper each partner makse a list of those things he/she has done or said that day or week which has harmed the relationship. On the other side of the paper each partner makes a list of those things our partner has done that was helpful to the relationship. These lists are then shared with each other. This step supports our spiritual growth. How have I harmed the relationship? How has my partner helped the relationship?

Daily practice of Step Ten maintains our honesty and humility and allows us to continue growing. When we think we are home free and comfortable, we may no longer see a need to attend meetings. We begin to find excuses (i.e., we are too tired, it's too far to drive, it's raining out, etc.). If we choose this path, we will eventually realize our relationship is in jeopardy. We may become irritable, short-tempered, negative thinking and relapse to old patterns of behavior (i.e., avoidance, working, spending, isolation, busyness, control, manipulation, withholding feelings, difficulty with intimacy).

Remember that nothing stays the same in our lives or coupleships. We are either growing one step at a time or regressing backward toward old behavior.

The program suggests three types of ongoing inventories:

1. Spot-check inventory (what are my underlying motives for what I am doing).

2. Daily inventory (usually a "question" done on the run or just before going to sleep).

3. Long-term periodic inventory (twice yearly spiritual retreat or reflection on how you have changed and what are necessary corrections).

Step 11

We sought through our common prayer and meditation to improve our conscious contact with God as we understood God, praying only for knowledge of God's will for us and the power to carry that out.

In Step Eleven, we have an opportunity to develop a deepening relationship with our Higher Power. In our relationship, this step is about our spiritual awakening. We are conscious. We improve our conscious contact with our Higher Power through prayer and meditation. The only requirement for a prayer to be successful is that it be sincere, humble, and not for our own selfish gain. Meditation is an ancient art of quieting the mind and <u>not</u> thinking. Some of us in our relationship find it difficult to sit quietly and

26

relax together free of mind chatter.

The miracle of this step is that we change the way we pray into a form of meditation. PRAYING ONLY FOR HIS/HER WILL FOR US.

When we are progressing with this step we will find a great sense of gratitude as a couple and a feeling of belonging and being worthy. We also get a sense of being guided and sustained as we work together as a couple.

Ultimate intimacy with your partner depends not only upon connecting emotionally, but also on connecting spiritually.

At this time it's good to look at your spiritual quest in Step Three and to review what you may want to add or change.

We need to spend time together daily as a couple--not just on vacation!

In becoming aware of the presence of our Higher Power, we also need to be aware of our own rhythms with our partner--our breathing patterns, waking, sleeping, lovemaking, and work patterns. Forget about demands for a few minutes and get quiet inside together. Share this.

If we have difficulty praying or lack experience with prayer and meditation, it is suggested that we use the Serenity Prayer.

God grant us the serenity...

Serenity meaning that we no longer recoil from the past, live in jeopardy because of our behavior now, or worry about the unknown future. We seek regular times to re-create ourselves and we avoid those times of depletion which make us vulnerable to despair and to old self-destructive patterns.

To accept the things we cannot change...

Accept change in that we not cause suffering for ourselves by clinging to that which no longer exists. All that we can count on is that nothing will be stable except how we respond to the transforming cycles in our lives of birth, growth, and death.

Courage to change the things we can...

Which means remembering that to give up our attempts to control outcomes does not require we give up our boundaries or our best efforts. It does mean our most honest appraisal of the limits of what we can do.

And the wisdom to know the difference...

Wisdom becomes the never-forgotten recognition of all those times when there was no way out, and new paths opened up like miracles in our lives.

Step 12

*Having had a spiritual awakening as the result of these
Steps, we tried to carry this message to other couples,
and to practice these principles in all aspects of our
lives, our relationship, and our families.*

Step Twelve is about taking the message of couple recovery to other couples. As in our individual programs, in the RCA fellowship we carried the message in many ways:

• *Sharing as a couple at recovery meetings.*

• *In coupleship, serving as meeting secretary-couple, treasurer, or greeter. Or we took the responsibility of literature couple, refreshment couple, intergroup representative, liaison couple, temporary and full-time sponsor couple.*

• *Mentioning RCA to others at retreats or in our individual program meetings and making a schedule of meetings available.*

• *Supporting the national convention through participation, voting as delegate, financial donation, or serving on the WSO Board.*

• *Writing our couple stories and sharing these with others.*

This step is meant for a lifetime. We get this program when we give it away. The results affect all of our relationships, and if we have children, we will be breaking the chains of addiction that have bound families for generations. We all learn from those couples who have gone before us. The message we carry is a liberating one. Working with newcomers can be a rewarding experience.

While we look forward to even more extensive program materials in the future, we hope that our experience, comments and suggestions above are helpful to you now. As always, just as in AA and other older fellowships, our experiences of how we work the Steps as couples will form the ongoing history of RCA. We eagerly anticipate your comments, suggestions, and questions.

The Twelve Traditions of RCA

Tradition 1

Our common welfare should come first;
couple recovery depends upon RCA unity.

We have seen that by working the 12 Steps of the RCA program, our coupleship has grown in commitment and intimacy. Now we must embark upon the 12 Traditions which provide guidance and direction for the RCA fellowship. The 12 Traditions must be understood and applied in order for the felowship to flourish and grow.

The "Traditions" are the glue and backbone of RCA itself. These 12 Traditions come to us through the program of Alcoholics Anonymous. We follow the Traditions to ensure the RCA fellowship will always be available for those couples who are recovering from multiple addictions which have affected their relationships.

Many of us have found that doing service has helped to speed our healing process. We have a new sense of belonging and we learn to work together with other couples and not "isolate" in our coupleships.

Before recovery, many of us thought we had the only "right" opinion and that only our viewpoints were correct. We learned in our group to listen to other couples. By serving the group, we learn many couples have differing opinions and viewpoints and we are able to listen without judgment. We learn to share time with each other and not monopolize the group with "oh, ain't it awful" stories. We choose topics and stay focused on the type of meeting which we are attending: couple chair, reflection, Steps, Traditions, topic or characteristics of functional couples. We enforce our safety guidelines and have the secretary couple responsive to act on the group's behalf as the trusted servants.

We have a responsibility to express ourselves--to give the program to others. We have experience, strength and hope in relationships to share. We have histories that may need to be heard. As a couple, we sometimes share just by listening and being present to hear another couple's story. However, if we consistently remain silent, it is not for the greater good of the group.

We may retain unity by having temporary sponsors for the first three meetings for newcomers. We may have "newcomer" meetings. We may have "newcomer" chips. We may share at the beginning of a meeting how RCA has been helpful to us. We may hand out a "newcomers" packet. Our RCA World Service Organization offers RCA Board approved literature.

RCA meetings nurture the relationship and provide opportunities to connect with our partner as well as with other couples. As we continue to show up, we learn from one another. We leave meetings with a sense of hope and of belonging. Our commitment expands from ourselves, to a Higher Power, to our partner in recovery, and to our group.

Our common need to be in a recovering relationship brought us to the front door of RCA. We need to safeguard our group's welfare, which gives to all us the stability and guidance we need to remain a part of the greater whole.

Tradition 2

For our group purpose there is but one ultimate authority—a loving God as known in our group conscience. Our leaders are but trusted servants; they do not govern.

When we look at the leaders (trusted servants) in our fellowship, we see secretaries, group treasurers, group contact couples, liaison couples to each region, and trustees to the World Service Board. We are aware that these couples are those who are willing to devote time, work and love to the RCA fellowship. These couples are dedicated to serving and not controlling or directing. The positions do not give authority to them, nor is there a chain of command or "mom & pop" couple.

Rotation of officers gives equal opportunity to serve, and puts the authority with our Higher Power. Everyone's vote counts. In this Tradition there is equality among all of us and we are reminded that equality belongs also in our family units. This Tradition brings about the importance of the 3-legged stool--communication, commitment and caring.

When there is difficulty in finding a couple to take a position, it is important not to allow one couple to continue doing the work because they are willing to do so. This couple can begin to feel very important and indispensable or even put upon or used. They can develop an attitude problem around management. Search for and encourage couples to volunteer for positions and perhaps even "share" the position with another couple. Maybe a 3-month term would be easier to fill than a 6-month term. Service gives the couple experience and growth in their relationship.

This Second Tradition will be valuable to those who sponsor other couples. It will prevent sponsors from assuming authority or responsibility over another's coupleship. Again the purpose is not to give advice or impose a decision or dictate an action about what's happening. The couple's sponsors agree to share their own experience, strength and hope. By providing feedback, the Sponsor Couple helps the other couple to see their options.

Longtime members may be helpful to a new group that is getting started. Often their guidance will set the structure of the meeting from the beginning and then other members can assume the leadership roles as they gain program knowledge and experience.

The group conscience is what governs the group, and we all help to form this conscience, by discussion. We set limits on holding office. We share the workload. We are autonomous and anonymous.

This wonderful Tradition protects and safeguards all of us and our group. Tradition 2 is deeply spiritual.

Tradition 3

The only requirement for RCA membership is a desire to remain in a committed relationship.

Tradition 3 tells us who we are and who is eligible to be in this fellowship. We are couples committed to restoring healthy communication, caring, and greater intimacy to our relationships. We suffer from many addictions and co-addictions; some identified and some not, some treated and some not. We also come from many levels of brokenness. Many of us have been separated or near divorce. Some of us are new in our relationships and seek to build intimacy as we grow together as couples.

Ultimately, we feel it is important for both members of a couple to be involved in individual recovery for real progress to be made in the relationship. It is not, however, a requirement to get started in couple recovery. RCA is a safe place to begin that healing process and it offers support for continued individual work.

We may refuse none who wish to recover, nor ought RCA membership ever depend upon money or conformity. Any two or three couples gathered together for restoring the commitment, communication and caring to their relationship may call themselves an RCA group, provided that, as a group, they have no other affiliation.

This Tradition helps us guard against "outsiders" who may see us as an audience for convenience, profit, or therapy. This does not limit us as individual couples from joining other organizations or seeking help for our own individual problems.

We as an RCA fellowship seek to keep the RCA focus.

Tradition 4

Each group should be autonomous except in matters affecting other groups or RCA as a whole.

Each RCA group should be responsible to no authority other than its own conscience. Our Traditions safeguard our program, guiding us and not controlling us, allowing us to act independently and reminding us to be ever mindful of our group as part of the whole fellowship. We are to conduct our work in the program according to the spiritual principles stated in the Traditions.

When RCA plans concern the welfare of neighboring groups also, those groups ought to be consulted. No group, regional committee, couple or individual should ever take any action that might affect RCA as a whole without conferring with the trustees of our World Service Organization Board. On such issues our common welfare is paramount. RCA is not an organization but a fellowship made up of couples in recovery.

Each group is responsible to conduct itself in a way that is good for the fellowship. RCA has suggested Safety Guidelines for the meetings and uses the suggested meeting format from its Big Book of RCA to conduct the meetings. It is also suggested that the local groups conduct business meetings once a month to maintain the good of the fellowship. Each group is free to choose its own meeting program and topics for discussion; to decide where and when it shall meet and how the funds will be apportioned. In a business meeting, discussion at length may be indicated. Minority opinions are to be aired and taken into consideration.

We are all responsible to make our program a program of attraction: to use the conference-approved literature from the World Service Organization and carry a unified message to the couples who are still suffering. We can do this by taking a meeting inventory. Each RCA group is responsible to take the time to know the Traditions and understand why they are important to the fellowship.

Tradition 5

Each group has but one primary purpose—to carry its message to recovering couples who still suffer.

Tradition 5 suggests that we will best be able to help other couples who are still suffering when we first help ourselves practice the 12 Steps. The 12 Steps give us the guidance we need to: 1) share our own experience, strength and hope with other couples, 2) give comfort to other couples, and 3) listen to other couples. Each Recovering Couples Anonymous group ought to be a spiritual entity HAVING BUT ONE PRIMARY PURPOSE--that of carrying its message of intimacy and commitment to couples who still suffer.

This Tradition sums up for us what our program is really about. Many couples come to RCA not knowing if they belong. In RCA we have a sampling of the "Characteristics of Dysfunctional Couples," which is a list to help couples identify problem areas in their relationships. Couples do not have to relate to all of these to admit their relationships are suffering or to seek help or guidance. The identification of such characteristics serves to let you know that "you are not alone" in your struggle to find intimacy.

The RCA philosophy lies within the 5th Tradition. RCA believes that a relationship, or coupleship, is like an infant, needing constant nurturing and care from both partners. It is important that each partner accept mutual responsibility for the problems or progress of the relationship, and furthermore, that each recognizes his/her individual recovery as an important factor for couple recovery.

RCA thinks of our lives in a relationship as being represented by a three-legged stool: our individual recovery, our partner's recovery, and our relationship recovery are all important "legs" to the serenity, stability, and intimacy we each seek.

When we welcome a newcomer couple to our fellowship, we extend to them a sharing of our experience, strength and hope. We extend to them a spiritual support and the opportunity to connect with other couples in the group through sponsorship, either temporary or long-term. We provide conference approved literature and a listing of meetings in the area with the opportunity to purchase or order the RCA Big Book, tapes from previous international conventions, and/or perhaps approved reading material from our meeting's library.

It is in the 5th Tradition that we truly reflect that in order to "get the program," we must "give it away!"

Tradition 6
RCA ought never endorse, finance, or lend the RCA name to any related facility or outside enterprise, lest problems of money, property, and prestige divert us from our primary purpose.

Tradition 5 stated the purpose of RCA--to carry its message to recovering couples who still suffer. Tradition 6 insures that we are not diverted from that purpose. Problems of money, property, and authority may easily divert us from our primary SPIRITUAL aim. We think, therefore, that any considerable property of genuine use to RCA, should be separately incorporated and managed, thus dividing the material from the spiritual. An RCA group, as such, should never go into business. Secondary aids to RCA, such as clubs, couples counseling entities or hospitals which require much property or administration, ought to be incorporated and so set apart that, if necessary, they can be freely discarded by the groups. Hence such facilities ought not to use the RCA name. Their management should be the sole responsibility of those people who financially support them. Hospitals and counseling entities ought to be well outside RCA and professionally supervised. While an RCA group may cooperate with anyone, such cooperation ought never go so far as affiliation or endorsement, actual or implied.

An RCA group can bind itself to no one. It has been our experience that RCA is an attraction to outside enterprises. They send members to us. RCA has a common bond with AA--that of recovery. This simply means that we should let the hospitals treat the sick, let the therapists do the counseling, and let the educators do the educating. We must not be diverted from our primary purpose.

Tradition 7

*Every RCA group should be fully self-supporting,
declining outside contributions.*

Being self-supporting is the RCA source of spiritual strength and self-respect. This Tradition places the financial responsibility for supporting our group on our own shoulders. We do not owe anyone any favors. We do not give certain people special treatment. We do not accept outside contributions. We do not sell our independence. We understand that we are responsible for our own survival and progress in recovery and we benefit with spiritual strength for our group.

The World Service Office is subject to this Tradition as well as the individual groups in Recovering Couples Anonymous. We think that any public solicitation of funds using the name of RCA is highly dangerous, whether by groups, clubs, therapy entities, hospitals, or outside agencies; that acceptance of gifts from any source, or of contributions carrying any obligations, is unwise.

We view with much concern those RCA treasuries which continue, beyond prudent reserves, to accumulate funds for no stated RCA purpose.
Experience has often warned us that nothing can so surely destroy our spiritual heritage as futile disputes over property, money, and authority.

In keeping with the 7th Tradition, the membership supports the World Service Organization by means of contributions by the groups, by individual donations and the sale of conference approved literature and other materials from WSO (i.e. chips, key chains, hats, bags, convention items, tapes, etc.). There are no dues or fees for membership. Voluntary contributions are collected when each meeting "practices the 7th Tradition" and a basket is passed. The financial pattern is simple, and this Tradition is the shortest.

Tradition 8

Recovering Couples Anonymous should remain forever non-professional, but our service centers may employ special workers.

Tradition 8 provides guidance to members who happen to be in the helping professions (counselors, clergy, physicians, social workers, nurses, etc.). Their exchanges at meetings should be about their own recovery in their own relationships and clearly they do not attend in their professional capacity or as experts in the field of intimacy and communication. We share our joy in the fellowship as couples, not as professionals. What we do for ourselves and others is not done for money or any material gain, but for our own spiritual growth.

Our World Service Office functions as a liaison center to foster the growth and unity for all RCA groups throughout the world. The WSO Office Manager is a contracted consultant position, and is accountable to the WSO Board of Trustees of the RCA Fellowship. RCA committee and subcommittee work is recognized as 12-Step service work. 12-Step work is non-professional and unpaid. WSO can hire persons as needed, e.g. clerical work, accounting, typesetting, etc.

Tradition 9

RCA, as such, ought never be organized; but we may create service boards or committees directly responsible to those they serve.

RCA, like AA, is a fellowship where there are no leaders but only trusted servants. The duties and terms of these servants are limited. Some of the positions you will seé will be the couple secretary, treasurer, literature persons, coffee people, temporary sponsors, greeters, and group contact couple. These positions rotate on a regular basis so that all couples involved have a chance to share responsibility. No couple directs and no couple controls the other members.

Our WSO Board of Trustees are directly responsible to the fellowship of RCA. In order to have the communications line open to other couples who are still suffering, we have our WSO office, which is incorporated and run by a contracted Office Manager. We also have Regional Liaison Couples (RLC) who serve designated parts of the country and world, and meet at the annual International Convention of RCA, the second weekend of August. These are couples who have made themselves available to help new groups being started. Each local group is encouraged to have a Group Contact Couple (GCC) who will bring information to the Regional Liaison Couple or to the Board. The fellowship of RCA is about the spirit of service, and so all couples are invited to volunteer themselves to service.

The "HAND IN HAND" newsletter is the official publication of RCA and is issued quarterly.

Tradition 10

Recovering Couples Anonymous has no opinion on outside issues: hence the RCA name ought never be drawn into public controversy.

No RCA group or member should ever, in such as way to implicate RCA, express any opinion on outside controversial issues--particularly those of politics, addiction reform or sectarian religion. Concerning such matters, they can express no view whatsoever. The Recovering Couples Anonymous groups oppose no one.

Tradition 11

Our public relations policy is based on attraction rather than on promotion; we need always maintain personal anonymity at the level of press, radio, TV, and films.

Tradition 11 is our guide whenever there is an opportunity to be public. This Tradition, like the others, is grounded in the spirituality of our program. We are reminded to preserve our anonymity. Public relations is ongoing in the program, as we reach out as couples to another couple and extend our hand and welcome them to our group.

When we desire to "carry the message," we provide information in the form of a list and location of meetings with only the first names of the couple and a telephone contact number. We may also leave an RCA information pamphlet on a bulletin board or at a treatment center to let other couples know that there is hope for intimacy in their relationships through a 12-Step program. Again, we preserve our anonymity with only a first name and contact number. We also have business cards with the WSO office number and fax number for anyone to call for additional information and literature.

Public relations in our RCA program is providing information to the public and reaching out couple to couple, with no thoughts of personal gain. There is never need to praise ourselves. When couples in RCA practice their recovery and live in the solution, they become more healthy and attractive. This in itself can elicit an attraction to the program from people who have seen a couple struggle before, and now see them with a sense of serenity and spirituality in their relationship.

It is under this Tradition that we, as couples, are able to speak freely and with confidence that nothing said in the meeting will leave the room. This Tradition is the practical application of the 1st Tradition, which says: "our common welfare should come first." To help insure the safety of the meeting, in addition to this understanding, we strive to obey the suggested Safety Guidelines. These are a reminder to all of us to again "create that safe environment where we can experience and share our pain."

Tradition 12

Anonymity is the spiritual foundation of all our Traditions, ever reminding us to place principles before personalities.

We of Recovering Couples Anonymous believe that the principle of anonymity has an immense spiritual significance. It reminds us that we are to place principles before personalities; that we are actually to practice a genuine humility. We can practice this humility by listening to other couples share their experience, strength, hope and pain in the meeting. Sometimes, in these meetings, we learned that even those couples we did not initially care for, frequently had ideas worth hearing. This Tradition shows us we can no longer afford judgments, based on whether or not we like that couple, to interfere with group cohesion.

Moved by the spirit of anonymity, we give up any desire for personal distinction as members of RCA and before the general public. We believe that each of us is responsible to take part in the protection and preservation of RCA as a whole in order to grow and work in unity.

God grant us the serenity...

Serenity meaning that we no longer recoil from the past, live in jeopardy because of our behavior now, or worry about the unknown future. We seek regular times to re-create ourselves and we avoid those times of depletion which make us vulnerable to despair and to old self-destructive patterns.

To accept the things we cannot change...

Accept change in that we not cause suffering for ourselves by clinging to that which no longer exists. All that we can count on is that nothing will be stable except how we respond to the transforming cycles in our lives of birth, growth, and death.

Courage to change the things we can...

Which means remembering that to give up our attempts to control outcomes does not require we give up our boundaries or our best efforts. It does mean our most honest appraisal of the limits of what we can do.

And the wisdom to know the difference...

Wisdom becomes the never-forgotten recognition of all those times when there was no way out, and new paths opened up like miracles in our lives.

Adaptation by Dr. Patrick Carnes

MEETING GUIDELINES

Suggested Guidelines for RCA Recovery Meetings

(Please adapt for your own group purposes.)

1. Pass out The Preamble, How It Works, The Twelve Steps, The Twelve Traditions, and The Promises for members to read. (Readings may include as well: The Reflections; Characteristics of Functional/ Dysfunctional Couples.)

2. "Welcome to the _____ meeting of Recovering Couples Anonymous. This is an (open/closed) meeting. Both singles and couples are welcome. (Or "This meeting is for couples only/closed to a special group," etc.)

   My name is _____ (give your name) and I'm a member of Recovering Couples Anonymous. "We hope you will find in this Fellowship the help and friendship we have been privileged to enjoy.

   Let's open the meeting with a moment of silence, followed by the Serenity Prayer. In this group, the Serenity Prayer uses the words we and us." (Group recites the Serenity Prayer.)

3. "A member will read the RCA Preamble." (Member does so.)

4. "A member will read How It Works." (Member does so.)

5. "A member will read the Twelve Steps of RCA." (Member does so.)

6. "A member will read the Tradition of the month. Or all Twelve Traditions, if this is your group's conscience." (Member does so.)

7. Optional readings. Groups usually seek to balance the time allocated for the various readings with the time allocated for couple-sharing.

8. "Now is the time we introduce ourselves as couples. I'm (give your name) and I'm part of this recovering couple. (Partner gives his/her name.) Please greet us as a couple." (The group greets the couple: "Hello, _____ and ____!") (Other meeting attendees give their names.)

9. "We will circulate our meeting's phone list. People who put their names on this list are willing to receive program calls. Phone calls are a helpful program tool. Leave your number if you like."

(Secretary-couple circulates the phone list.)

10. Rules of the house, (e.g., no smoking, where to park, safety guidelines about cross-talk, literature, bathrooms, coffee, etc.)

11. "The format of these meetings is _____. (Monthly format: Speaker Couple one week; Step Study another week; Reflections the third week; etc.) "The format of tonight's meeting is _____."
(Secretary announces the format.)

12. "This is the time for sharing our experience, strength, and hope. If one member of a couple shares, the other member may share next if she or he chooses. Please keep your sharing brief. We ask that we avoid cross-talk. Avoiding cross-talk means that when we speak, we address the meeting as a whole."

13. If this is a Speaker Couple meeting, the Secretary says, "The Speakers will have about ten minutes each to share on a topic they have chosen. Now let's welcome our speakers for tonight." (Secretary introduces Speakers.) If this is a Step Study/Reflection/Tradition meeting, the Secretary asks whoever has the Step/Reflection/Tradition to read; then the Secretary opens up the meeting for sharing. "Will whoever has the particular reading please read it and then the meeting will be open for sharing."

14. Speakers speak, and/or members share.

15. At about 15 minutes before closing, the Secretary may say, "Would any of our newcomers wish to share? Or anyone with a real need to share?"

16. The Secretary ends the sharing at five (5) minutes before the close of the meeting.

17. "Now we practice the Seventh Tradition, which states that Every RCA group ought to be fully self-supporting, declining outside contributions. Our contributions go for rent and literature, and for support of our World Service Organization."

18. If this has been a Speaker Couple meeting, the Secretary says, "Let's thank our Speakers."

19. Announcements: "It's time for RCA announcements and other 12-Step-related announcements. Our next business meeting will be _____.
Are there any other RCA-related announcements or any other recovery-related announcements?" Members give their announcements.

20. "A member will now read The Promises."
    Member does so. Secretary distributes copies of The Unity Prayer.

21. "Let's end our meeting with The Unity Prayer." *(*Or the Serenity Prayer or another prayer.)

The meeting is now over.

SUGGESTED MEETING TOPICS

Issues For Recovering Couples

We have developed 12 presuppositions about couples who are in recovery. The following is a brief outline:

1. *Couples are a oneness.* Together two people who are in a committed relationship form a coupleship, a oneness, a distinct and separate entity. This coupleship has a life of its own and needs to be nurtured appropriately. Couple recovery depends on this nurturance. Both partners in a relationship need individual recovery: meetings, sponsors, therapy, a support group, spirituality, recreation, vocation, and other individual interests. A coupleship needs these same elements for couple recovery.

There are, then, three elements of couple recovery. Our individual recoveries are the two basic components. Our coupleship's recovery is the third component. One of the symbols of RCA is the three-legged stool. Each leg represents one of these components. If one leg is missing, the stool will fall. If one component is missing, the relationship will fail.

This is why, for example, many of us know how hard it is for one partner to be identified as the addict and in recovery while the other partner has no individual recovery. One partner grows and the other doesn't. Individual recovery for only one partner will, therefore, produce more distance in the relationship.

2. *In addictive relationships, the partner of a primary addict is referred to as the co-addict.* Addiction theory suggests that this person is often a co-dependent and/or an enabler. Some co-addicts have assumed that if the addict gets sober they will no longer be co-addicts. This is not true. Co-addiction is a disease in and of itself. Co-addicts grow up in families where they learn to cope with addictions of all kinds on the part of other family members. They may find that throughout their lives they related to a series of addicts. Their current partner is just another in a long list. They make a choice to be with their current partner for good reasons. They will not get well just because their partner is recovering. Being in relationship with an addict is normal for them.

Co-addicts should, therefore, be in recovery for themselves. Sobriety becomes learning healthy self-nurture, boundaries, and individuality.

Co-addicts may have their own primary addiction(s). It is not uncommon that two addicts are in relationship and are co-addicted to each other. Each one might historically claim that his or her addiction is fueled by trying to cope with his or her partner. This is not true.

3. Both partners must accept responsibility for the health or disease of their relationship. Each of us brings our own addictions, personalities, family-of-origin messages, and various individual dysfunctions into the relationship. The relationship doesn't create them. The elements brought by both partners contribute to the nature of the relationship.

This does not mean that we are responsible for any addictive or dysfunctional behavior on our partner's part. Those behaviors are his/her responsibility and reflect choices that he/she makes in order to cope with feelings (including the feelings generated by the state of the relationship). Both of us are responsible for the presence or absence of intimacy between us.

As soon as each of us accepts mutual responsibility, we are ready for the First Step of RCA: "__We__ admitted that __we__ were powerless over __our__ relationship and that __our__ life together had become unmanageable."

4. Both partners may be co-dependent. This factor may be an aspect of our co-addiction with each other. Partner codependency is really based on profound fear of abandonment, deep shame, and a strong need for approval. Enmeshed partner attachments may result and we may seek to control our partner and prevent him/her from leaving.

There can be two basic styles of this control. In one style, we seek to manipulate our partner by always doing what we think he/she needs or wants. As this kind of co-dependent, we would almost literally die for our partner. This style might also include a victim stance which projects an image of being such a poor, wretched, mistreated person that no one would ever leave us.

The other style is a more directly manipulative one. In this style, we use anger, orders, argumentation, and/or the suggestion (in a variety of subtle and not-so-subtle ways) that we are superior and should control the behavior of our partner. This is still codependency in that it is based on the deep fear of our partner leaving.

Addictive relationships are codependent ones. Each of us fears the other leaving, and we both use our own personal co-dependent style to seek to prevent this from happening.

5. Both partners probably suffer from intimacy disorder. Intimacy disorder is based on the individual feeling of shame that says, "If you really knew me, you would hate me." Intimacy disorder produces a fear of intimacy and an inability to be honest and vulnerable with our partner.

One of the maxims of intimacy disorder is that we will be least honest with the person we are most afraid of losing. Many of us experience great resentment because our partner seems to be able to be totally honest with relative strangers but not with us. We need to realize that we may be the last one to know, not because our partner is willingly trying to deceive us or because he/she doesn't care, but because he/she is deathly afraid of losing us.

43

Ultimately, intimacy is a matter of practice. We must learn to take great risks to tell the truth about ourselves, the truth about old behaviors, feelings, attitudes, preferences, and needs.

As we take these risks we will find that our partners usually don't leave, but that they are grateful for our honesty. Practicing like this will build trust and intimacy.

6. Both partners usually have significant family-of-origin issues.
The limited amount of research that has been conducted with addicted couples would suggest that each of us is a victim of some kind of abuse. Addicted couples learn unhealthy styles of relationship in their families. We don't receive healthy modeling of intimacy and nurturing.

Each of us may be the victim of invasive abuse in which our personal boundaries have been violated emotionally, physically, sexually, or spiritually. Such abuse creates suppressed anger and rage, and profound fear and anxiety. Addictions may develop as ways of coping with these feelings.

Each of us may also be the victim of abandonment abuse, in which our needs for nurturing were not met by one or both of our parents (or primary caretakers). This form of abuse leaves deep holes which are full of great loneliness.

We may suppress memories of and feelings about invasive abuse. The feelings, however, can be provoked without the memories becoming conscious. Our partner may say or do something that reminds us of our abuse. This may produce the old but buried feelings. The reactions, such as anger, that occur may seem out of proportion to the current event. Many couples, for example, fight over trivial matters. Our rage or sadness may seem totally inappropriate. We may get mad at our partner for over-reacting. Unsolved arguments and "mysterious" emotional reactions can often be traced to family-of-origin issues. We can learn to be patient with each other and help each other trace back to the roots of these feelings.

Abandonment abuse creates the codependency that is described in point four. It is based on fear of current abandonment. Often one of us hopes that our partner will solve the feeling of abandonment. We may think that our partner will be the nurturing parent we never had. We may hear ourselves saying, "I'm not your mother (or father)."

No partner can ever take the place of a parent. When we realize this fact, pressure is taken off our partner to be someone he/she can never be. True partner intimacy can then proceed.

7. In order to stay together, one partner or both partners may need to divorce their parents. This assumes that one or both of our parents is/are the abusers. If the abuse has been invasive, we will need to create boundaries around the abusive parent. This can mean a variety of things, from not being able to see or talk to that parent, to limits on the frequency or nature of visits. This will be particularly true if there is fear that the parent will continue the pattern of abuse with grandchildren.

If the abuse has been abandonment, we will need to grieve the loss. This might involve significant amounts of counseling and/or group support. Grief work must be verbalized. When this happens over time, pressure will be taken off the our partner to be the perfect nurturer.

If we can divorce our abusive parents, we won't need to divorce each other.

8. *Addicted couples are full of illusions about ideal relationships.* We will have a list of characteristics of what makes an ideal couple. For example, we may think that an ideal couple never violates vows, has a certain amount of money, perfect kids, etc. Sometimes this list is fueled by religious values. For example, a couple might think that "The sun should never set on our anger." Such a couple might argue well into the night trying to get it right.

A couple should make a list of these ideals. Some of them will be totally unrealistic. Perhaps, for example, we will never obtain the money we thought we would have, or our kids will never be perfect. We must let go of these ideals and perhaps grieve over them. Some of the list can be reclaimed. Wedding or commitment vows can be rededicated. Perhaps other ideals are also realistic but require work to obtain. Some of the ideals may require help to achieve. Perhaps it is realistic to have a certain amount of money, but our coupleship will need help to set budgets, balance the checkbook, or make wise investments. This help can even take the form of specific sponsors for these goals, such as a financial sponsor-couple.

9. *Just as an individual addict has slips, so will a couple.* An individual in recovery knows that he/she must maintain his/her program, that addiction is a lifetime disease. Likewise as a recovering couple, we must maintain our program for life. If we don't, old patterns of dysfunction will return.

Slips happen to couples when our communication breaks down, when old fights and patterns of interaction take place again, and when we start distancing from each other. As couples in recovery, we have a sense of this-that our intimacy is breaking down. If we can listen to ourselves at these times we will recognize that an old and familiar loneliness returns to us, angers and resentments are resurrected, and fear of abandonment is elevated.

When we start to distance, old individual patterns of addiction may be the way in which we do so. A symptom of the distancing may be that one of us criticizes some of these old addictive patterns, which in turn may cause our partner to further distance. This creates a couple addictive cycle and causes us to further distance from each other.

At these times we need to remember to practice the tools of recovery. The aid of our sponsoring couple should be enlisted, meetings should be attended, and our contracts resurrected and re-examined. If the slip has become really deep, we can see a counselor. Slips may mean that old family-of-origin issues have surfaced. If this is true, we can seek individual counseling.

If our individual addictions have also surfaced as a method of coping, then our individual recovery tools must be employed.

10. There will be little social support for the relationship. We have found that when a couple gets into recovery, the social system around them may not understand the changes or support them. Certainly families which are not in recovery will have an investment in maintaining the old ways of interaction. They might discourage any changes. For example, one couple changed their anniversary date after having recommitted their vows. Their parents and other family members could not grasp this change and refused to recognize it. Many of us also receive passive-aggressive comments or questions about our recovery. This dynamic may include our children. If they have grown used to their relationship to us in dysfunction, then recovery changes, which bring us closer together and cause us to spend more time together, might be hard for them. Some of us, in our loneliness, might have spent more time with a child. The need for this might stop in recovery. Children can demonstrate behaviors which indicate their fear of abandonment when their parents get into recovery. Obviously, we need to assure our children that they are still loved and give them special time and attention.

Old friendships, formed during our addictive days, also may not understand the changes in us. Conversations with them become like speaking Greek. They seem superficial. These friendships might also lead toward old addictive patterns. We don't want necessarily to do away with old friends, but we may need to be careful. We will find that new recovering friends will be the ones we gravitate toward.

Social and economic conditions may not be supportive of couple recovery. For example, we may face a situation in which both partners need to work. Time for the relationship may be at a premium. If we are trying to share responsibilities around the home or the care of the children, employers may not understand a need for creative scheduling. Old debts or economic concerns may threaten us and raise old issues. Ultimately a recovering couple must be ready to go to any length to recover. This could mean a willingness to make any lifestyle changes we need in order to survive. We might also need to grieve the loss of family support, friendships, and even jobs, houses, or communities.

11. If a couple doesn't work on their relationship, the same issues will surface with different partners in the next relationship. This means that we must practice couple recovery with our partner. Many of us had many years of individual recovery in place when we met our partner. Our couple issues were the same when we got into the relationship as the ones we experienced in previous relationships.

Divorce or separation and individual recovery are not answers to couple problems. We may be the strongest person possible, but our relationship issues will be the same until they encounter healing in relationship. This does not mean that we should stay in a relationship at all costs. If our partner can't participate mutually in recovery and if the relationship is destructive, it might be a matter of emotional and/or physical safety to get out.

12. Couples will experience shame just as individuals do. This is called "coupleshame." We must be aware that our individual shame gets doubled in relationship when we become convinced that we are a terrible couple. We are terrible friends, parents, sexual partners, managers of money, communicators, etc. We can think that we are in the worst relationship imaginable. The only solution seems to be to end the relationship.

The answer for coupleshame is the same as for individual shame. We must tell our story to other couples and experience that we are not alone in our problems. In this way we also can experience affirmation for ourselves as couples. Gradually over time our relationship will heal and we will experience gifts of intimacy that few other couples know. In these ways our shame will heal.

If we understand these principles of addictive couples, we can also reduce our shame. Since we come from dysfunctional families, is it any wonder that we have had imperfect relationships? We learn to give ourselves a break. We have done the best that we could. Greater gifts of loving are possible, but only as we practice the Steps and grow together in our recovery.

Some Deadly Issues

We have found that addicted couples fight and get into serious trouble around a number of common issues. Not all couples will have all of them, but most will have some. The following is just a list and is not necessarily in any particular order.

1. Sex

2. Money

3. Kids

4. Roles, Rules and Boundaries

5. Trust

6. Past Behaviors

7. Controlling Partner's Slips

8. Partner's Family

9. Unfair Fighting

10. Not Having Mutual Interests

Characteristics of Functional and Dysfunctional Couples

1. *Dysfunctional:* Being together and unhappy is safer than being alone.

   Functional: **Being together brings us joy and happiness.**

2. *Dysfunctional:* It is safer to be with other people than it is to be alone and intimate with our partner.

   Functional: **Being alone and intimate with our partner is as safe as being with other people.**

3. *Dysfunctional:* If I really let my partner know what I've done or what I'm feeling and thinking (who I am), s/he will leave me.

   Functional: **When I really let my partner know what I've done or what I'm thinking (who I am), it increases our intimacy. It's met with acceptance.**

4. *Dysfunctional:* It is easier to hide (medicate) our feelings through addictive/compulsive behavior than it is to express them.

   Functional: **We no longer need to hide and medicate our feelings through our addictive/compulsive behavior. We can express our feelings.**

5. *Dysfunctional:* Being enmeshed and totally dependent with each other is perceived as being in love.

   Functional: **Being interdependent adds strength to the relationship.**

6. *Dysfunctional:* We find it difficult to ask for what we need, both individually and as a couple.

   Functional: **We are learning to ask for what we need, both individually and a couple.**

49

7. *Dysfunctional:* Being sexual is equal to being intimate.

   Functional: **Being sexual enhances our relationship (increases our intimacy).**

8. *Dysfunctional:* We either avoid our problems or feel we are individually responsible for solving the problems we have as a couple.

   Functional: **We are learning to face our problems and not to feel individually responsible for solving the problems we have as a couple.**

9. *Dysfunctional:* We believe that we must agree on everything.

   Functional: **We believe we don't have to agree on everything.**

10. *Dysfunctional:* We believe that we must enjoy the same things and have the same interests.

    Functional: **We believe we can have different interests and enjoy different things and enjoy being together.**

11. *Dysfunctional:* We believe that to be a good couple we must be socially acceptable.

    Functional: **We don't have to be socially acceptable.**

12. *Dysfunctional:* We have forgotten how to play together.

    Functional: **We can play and have fun together.**

13. *Dysfunctional:* It is safer to get upset about little issues than to express our true feelings about larger ones.

    Functional: **We are learning to express our true feelings about larger issues, and we are learning to resolve conflict.**

14. *Dysfunctional:* It is easier to blame our partners than it is to accept our own responsibility.

    Functional: We are learning to accept our individual responsibility.

15. *Dysfunctional:* We deal with conflict by getting totally out of control or by not arguing at all.

    Functional: We are learning to deal with conflict and to fight fairly.

16. *Dysfunctional:* We experience ourselves as inadequate parents.

    Functional: We accept our limitations as parents.

17. *Dysfunctional:* We are ashamed of ourselves as a couple.

    Functional: We are proud of ourselves as a couple.

18. *Dysfunctional:* We repeat patterns of dysfunction from our families-of-origin.

    Functional: We are recognizing and breaking the patterns of dysfunction from our families-of-origin.

TOOLS OF RECOVERY
Adapted with permission of Workaholics Anonymous.

We find these recovery tools useful for restoring and then sustaining the commitment, intimacy, and joy in our relationship.

1. **MEETINGS:** We attend RCA meetings to learn how the Program works, and to share our experiences, strengths, and hopes with other couples. In meetings we learn that our struggles and troubles are not unique, and we gain the hope and assurance that our own coupleship can recover and grow. Meetings often bring couples closer and encourage communication.

2. **SHARING AT MEETINGS:** Being honest and vulnerable in front of our partners is frightening but worth it. Many of us believe that our relationships recover in direct proportion to our willingness to share at meetings.

3. **TELEPHONING:** We use the phone to contact members of our Fellowship between meetings. Sometimes we "book-end" a critical coupleship decision or coupleship activity between two strength-giving phone calls.

4. **CALLING A MORATORIUM:** When communications break down, a prior agreement to call a moratorium for 15 minutes, an hour, or a day can interrupt destructive interaction. We can walk away from each other but not from the relationship.

5. **DEVELOPING A SUPPORT SYSTEM INDIVIDUALLY AND AS A COUPLE:** Meeting with other couples over coffee to discuss our conflicts shows that we are not alone and allows us to get another perspective on our problems.

6. **READING AND WORKING THE STEPS:** Recovering Couples Anonymous is first and foremost a 12-step Program. Couples can apply the Steps to relationships either as individuals or as partners. The principles and techniques which helped restore our lives to sanity and bring a measure of serenity to us as individuals can work for us as a couple.

7. **SPONSORSHIP:** As part of the surrender process, we admit our weaknesses as individuals and as a couple. And we ask others for help, including our RCA sponsors as well as other members in the RCA Program. Acting as sponsors for other couples helps bring our coupleship closer. Helping others focus on their relationship can help us see where our own relationship has been and where it is to go.

8. **LISTENING AND COMMUNICATING:** We set aside a time each day for hearing each other's comments, feelings, and gratitude. Before accepting any major couple commitments in our relationship, we consult and listen to our Higher Power for guidance. We are learning to practice "fair fighting" by developing our own "Fighting Contract."

9. **BALANCING:** To help build balance in our relationship, each day we remember to develop personal relationships with persons other than just our partner. And each day we remember to nourish our spiritual growth together, our creativity, and our playful attitudes.

10. **CALLING A MEETING OF TWO:** Either partner can call a meeting of two at any time, anywhere. A structure of raising hands, no cross-talk, and closing with the Serenity Prayer guarantees being heard and often helps us regain our sense of humor.

11. **READING DAILY LITERATURE:** Daily reading of literature can help keep the focus on recovery.

12. **SERVICE:** We readily extend help to other couples, knowing that assistance to others adds to the quality of our own relationship recovery. We seek out and accept joint service positions in RCA such as meeting secretaries, treasurers, coffee-makers, and phone-tree chairpersons; we find that doing service together builds our sense of joint participation in our relationship and in its recovery.

MEETING FORMAT

THE SERENITY PRAYER
God, grant us the serenity

To accept the things we cannot change,

Courage to change the things we can,

And wisdom to know the difference.

PREAMBLE

Ours is a fellowship of recovering couples. We suffer from many different addictions, and we share our experience, strength, and hope with each other that we may solve our common problems and help other recovering couples restore their relationships. The only requirement for membership is a desire to remain committed to each other and to develop new intimacy. There are no dues or fees for membership; we are self-supporting through our own contributions. We are not allied with any organization. We do not wish to engage in any controversy, neither endorse nor oppose any causes. Although there is no organizational affiliation between Alcoholics Anonymous and our fellowship, we are based on the principle of AA. Our primary purpose is to stay committed in loving and intimate relationships and to help other couples achieve freedom from addicted and destructive relationships.

HOW IT WORKS

Rarely have we seen a couple fail who have thoroughly followed our path. Those who do not recover are people who cannot or will not completely give themselves to this simple program. They are naturally incapable of grasping and developing a manner of living which demands mutual and rigorous honesty. There are those, too, who cannot or will not make a commitment to their partners. There are those who suffer from grave emotional and mental disorders, but many of them do recover if they have the capacity to be honest.

Our stories disclose in a general way what we used to be like, what happened, and what we are like now. If you have decided you want what we have and are willing to go to any length to get it, then you are ready to take certain steps.

At some of these we balked. We thought we could find an easier, softer way. But we could not. With all the earnestness at our command, we beg of you to be fearless and thorough from the start. Some of us have tried to hold on to our old ideas, and the result was nil until we let go absolutely.

Remember that we deal with addictions-cunning, baffling, powerful. We also deal with all those memories of past hurts, misbehavior, and vows violated. Without help our anger, hurt, and mistrust are too great for us. But there is one who has all power; that one is God. May you find God now.

Half measures availed us nothing. We stood at the turning point. We asked God's protection and care with complete abandon.

Here are the steps we took, which are suggested as a program of recovery.

THE TWELVE STEPS OF RCA

Adapted with permission of Alcoholics Anonymous World Services, Inc.

1. We admitted we were powerless over our relationship and that our life together had become unmanageable.

2. We came to believe that a power greater than ourselves could restore us to commitment and intimacy.

3. We made a decision to turn our wills and our life together over to the care of God as we understood God.

4. We made a searching and fearless moral inventory of our relationship together as a couple.

5. We admitted to God, to each other, and to another couple the exact nature of our wrongs.

6. We were entirely ready to have God remove all these defects of character, communication, and caring.

7. We humbly asked God to remove our shortcomings.

8. We made a list of all persons we had harmed and became willing to make amends to them all.

9. We made direct amends to such people wherever possible, except when to do so would injure them or others.

10. We continued to take personal inventory and when we were wrong promptly admitted it to our partner and to others we had harmed.

11. We sought through our common prayer and meditation to improve our conscious contact with God as we understood God, praying only for knowledge of God's will for us and the power to carry that out.

12. Having had a spiritual awakening as the result of these Steps, we tried to carry this message to other couples, and to practice these principles in all aspects of our lives, our relationship, and our families.

THE TWELVE STEPS OF ALCOHOLICS ANONYMOUS

1. We admitted we were powerless over alcohol-that our lives had become unmanageable. 2. Came to believe that a Power greater than ourselves could restore us to sanity. 3. Made a decision to turn our will and our lives over to the care of God as we understood Him. 4. Made a searching and fearless moral inventory of ourselves. 5. Admitted to God, to ourselves, and to another human being the exact nature of our wrongs. 6. Were entirely ready to have God remove all these defects of character. 7. Humbly asked Him to remove our shortcomings. 8. Made a list of all persons we had harmed, and became willing to make amends to them all. 9. Made direct amends to such people wherever possible, except when to do so would injure them or others. 10. Continued to take personal inventory and when we were wrong promptly admitted it. 11. Sought through prayer and meditation to improve our conscious contact with God as we understood Him, praying only for knowledge of His will for us and the power to carry that out. 12. Having had a spiritual awakening as the result of these steps, we tried to carry this message to alcoholics, and to practice these principles in all our affairs. (Used with permission of Alcoholics Anonymous World Services, Inc.)

HOW IT WORKS
(Part Two)

Many of us exclaimed, "What an order! We can't go through with it. Our love is lost, our vows forever violated, our communication destroyed, our families broken beyond repair."

Do not be discouraged. No couple among us has been able to maintain anything like perfect adherence to these principles.

We are not saints, our love is not perfect, our energy not unbounded, nor our relationships ideal. There is no such thing as the ultimately caring and nurturing partner or perfect intimacy.

The point is that we are willing to grow together along spiritual lines. The principles we have set down are guides to progress. We claim spiritual progress rather than spiritual perfection. In our spirituality we claim the goal of greater caring, communication, and intimacy.

Our understanding of our addictions and our personal histories before and after recovery make clear three pertinent ideas:

1. That as addicts our commitment had become unmanageable. That despite our best efforts we were headed for separation and/or divorce.

2. That probably no human power could have restored us to commitment and intimacy.

3. That God could and would if God were sought.

THE TWELVE TRADITIONS OF RCA

1. Our common welfare should come first; couple recovery depends upon RCA unity.

2. For our group purpose there is but one ultimate authority, a loving God as known in our group conscience. Our leaders are but trusted servants; they do not govern.

3. The only requirement for RCA membership is a desire to remain in a committed relationship.

4. Each group should be autonomous except in matters affecting other groups or RCA as a whole.

5. Each group has but one primary purpose to carry its message to recovering couples who still suffer.

6. RCA ought never endorse, finance, or lend the RCA name to any related facility or outside enterprise, lest problems of money, property, and prestige divert us from our primary purpose.

7. Every RCA group should be fully self-supporting, declining outside contributions.

8. Recovering Couples Anonymous should remain forever nonprofessional, but our service centers may employ special workers.

9. RCA, as such, ought never be organized; but we may create service boards or committees directly responsible to those they serve.

10. Recovering Couples Anonymous has no opinion on outside issues; hence the RCA name ought never be drawn into public controversy.

11. Our public relations policy is based on attraction rather than promotion; we need always maintain personal anonymity at the level of press, radio, TV, and films.

12. Anonymity is the spiritual foundation of all our traditions, ever reminding us to place principles before personalities.

SAFETY GUIDELINES
Suggested RCA Meeting Safety Guidelines

Anonymity and mutual respect of boundaries are essential to providing a healing experience to each of us. Most of us have had great difficulty establishing our boundaries, assertiveness, and personal space. We are sensitive to crosstalk. Our purpose is not to give advice or try to fix one another, but rather to create a safe environment where we can experience and share our pain. We have found that:

1. It is OK to feel.

2. It is OK to make mistakes.

3. It is OK to have respectful conflict.

4. It is OK to have needs and ask for them to be met.

5. It is important to respect others (partners and others in the group). It is important to avoid self-righteous statements, baiting or button-pushing statements, case-building statements, and the taking or sharing of another person's inventory.

6. It is important to respect ourselves and to avoid self put-downs and self-pity. It is helpful to take ownership of our own story and to take credit for our progress and work in recovery.

7. Anonymity is our spiritual foundation. Who you see here, what you hear here, when you leave here, let it stay here.

We have care and concern for ourselves and for our coupleships. We meet to both receive and provide the nurturing our relationships need to grow and endure. For that reason, it is important for us to act and speak respectfully to our partners and others. As we do this, we value the group and the relationships within it.

THE PROMISES

If we are honest about our commitment and painstaking about working the Twelve Steps together, we will quickly be amazed at how soon our love returns. We are going to know a new freedom and a new happiness. We will learn how to play and have fun together. As we experience mutual forgiveness we will not regret the past nor wish to shut the door on it. Trust in each other will return. We will comprehend the word serenity, and we will know peace.

No matter how close to brokenness we have come, we will see how our experiences can benefit others. That feeling of uselessness, shame, and self-pity will disappear. We will lose interest in selfish things and gain interest in our partners, families, and others. Self-seeking will slip away. Our whole attitude and outlook on life will change. Fear of people and of economic insecurity will leave us. We will intuitively know how to handle situations which used to baffle us. We will be better parents, workers, helpers, and friends. We will suddenly realize that God is doing for us what we could not do for ourselves.

Are these extravagant promises? We think not. They are being fulfilled among us sometimes quickly, sometimes slowly. They will always materialize if we work for them.

For those of you who are new to our fellowship, there are no problems that you have experienced that are not common to many of us.

Just as our love for our partners has been imperfect, we may not always be adequately able to express to you the deep love and acceptance we feel for you. Keep coming back, the process of loving and communication grows in us and with each other one day at a time.

Remember always, what is said here stays here. Will those of you who are willing, join us in the closing prayer (Unity Prayer, Serenity Prayer, Lord's Prayer, etc.)

THE FOUNDERS' FIRST STEP STORIES

In the first edition of the Big Book, we decided to include only the First Step stories of the three founding couples. Our hope was that they would serve as examples, and that they would inspire others to write and submit their coupleship stories for inclusion in future editions. That hope has been realized. It is also our hope eventually to have written examples of all of the steps.

Step One-We admitted that we were powerless over our relationship and that our life together had become unmanageable.

Mark and Deb L.

Our first step [story] began in our families-of-origin. They determined whom we would look for in a partner as we began to date. We met early in that process while still in high school.

Mark was raised in a minister's home. His father was extremely strong and controlling emotionally, a very public person, admired greatly by the congregations he served. His mother was extremely passive, quiet, and shame-filled. While Mark's dad had little trouble sharing his thoughts and feelings, usually with religious interpretations and without boundaries, his mom usually talked to no one and shared almost nothing about herself.

Mark's perception of his parents is that they talked of superficial things with each other, with his dad always dominating conversations with his thoughts. The life and business of the church was the life of the family. His parents didn't seem affectionate toward one another, either emotionally or physically. They were lonely even when with each other but didn't consciously recognize or accept it.

Mark became a sexual abuse victim, some of which he remembers, some of which he "knows" took place before the age of three. He was also an emotional incest victim. His dad expected him to be his "buddy" and to be available to him for many activities and conversations. In this process his dad was grooming Mark to be just like himself--a minister--and taught Mark that people in power can bend the rules, including exploiting others. His mom let this happen--even encouraged it as she abandoned Mark emotionally.

Mark was looking for a woman he could dominate emotionally and sexually, one who would be perfectly nurturing physically and sexually, but who would also be submissive and passive. Although he did not know it, he was lonely and longed for a deeper emotional relationship, but he didn't have any tools to ask for it. He was also afraid of a strong woman--afraid that she would leave him if she really knew him. Mark was also looking for a woman from a social and economic background which would correct his image of his family being poor.

60

Deb has a twin sister and an older brother. Deb was raised in the home of an executive who is very successful and popular, a "good guy" everybody likes. With all this he is very concerned with money and security, taking care of things so that nothing "bad" will happen. He is very protective. He is a gentle man, oriented around his family to a fault. He is also generally affirming and supportive. There is, however, a loneliness about him that we sense especially now that we're in recovery. There was certainly no ability to share emotionally in Deb's family. Her parents taught her the attitude that if you worked hard everything would work out all right. There were always solutions to everything. Deb had polio at age three; she doesn't remember anyone talking to her about how painful and frightening it was.

Deb's mother was a trained professional who stopped her career when she married. She was an only child and was moved numerous times as a youth and teenager. While she played a traditional domestic female role, she was extremely strong-willed and opinionated. She learned how to control her own fears and insecurities and passed down a general inability to deal with them. She did not discuss sexual things, but she passed on clear messages, instilling in Deb a general fear of one's body and of men.

Deb's twin sister was very socially and athletically outgoing. Deb also perceived her as more physically attractive as well as more popular. Deb took a back seat in many ways while growing up. She became an exceptional student and organizer and was very successful at school in various activities. A major social victory for her was becoming a cheerleader as a junior and senior.

Although Deb's family attended church, religion was rarely discussed. Deb would often go to youth groups and church on her own. When she was a senior, her family began attending the church that Mark's dad served.

Deb feels she was abandoned emotionally and spiritually, that she was taught a general workaholic lifestyle and to fear problems but not talk about them. She was also instilled with traditional sexist values and roles, with dislike of her body, and a fear of sex. Despite all of this, she brought a strong family-centered orientation to her relationship with Mark.

Deb was looking for a man who was socially outgoing and religious (when she first started dating Mark, one of her favorite songs was "The Only Boy Who Could Ever Move Me Was the Son of a Preacher Man"). She also was lonely, but didn't know anything about sharing feelings.

We started dating during the late sixties while Mark was in college and Deb a high school senior. Previous to this we had known each other from afar. Friends of ours who were dating each other set us up. This is significant in that this couple later married, and we came to be totally enmeshed with them as a couple later in our own marriage.

We dated for four years while we pursued our education at separate campuses. Ours was a relationship of weekend visits, telephone calls, letters, and summers at home. The alone time served to heighten the "absence makes the heart grow fonder" effect. For Mark, his abandonment issues

61

with his mother made him pursue visits, calls, and letters rather fanatically. For example, in just two years, he made over sixty six-hour round-trip visits to see Deb at her campus.

We are now conscious that we sacrificed a lot of campus social opportunities and other activities to see each other so much and to be "faithful" to each other. Deb is also aware that she sacrificed career interests she might have had in order to prepare herself adequately for the role of minister's wife. Mark had "decided" to enter the ministry (actually he was following the incest script that he had been given). The fact that Deb sacrificed her interests to support Mark's career is an ongoing source of grief for her. It also angers her to know that Mark was pursuing some of this out of obligation and not out of a sense of what he really wanted to do.

We both had been "programmed" to go to and stay in college. We were on separate campuses and felt like we "wanted" to get married as soon as possible. This led us to accelerate our pace, and we both graduated in three years. We were married during Mark's Christmas break from seminary.

While others around us participated in the sexual revolution, we had not. Though we had read Masters and Johnson and "knew" a lot, we were both virgins when we got married. Of course we each had quite different expectations regarding frequency of love-making after we started living together. These different expectations were a constant source of tension that we felt but never talked about. We played many silent games around these expectations.

Also, as Mark prepared to enter the ministry, both of us were growing uncomfortable with the roles we knew the ministry would bring, but we didn't know how to talk about it. Mark's solution was to enter graduate school and work towards a Ph.D. in the field of pastoral care. So we went off to a new town. Mark worked part-time at a church and Deb, who had prepared as a home economics teacher, taught for one year in a totally frustrating situation. The expectation was--again--that Deb would work while Mark pursued his career.

The frustrations in our communication, work, and sexual lives were mostly unrecognized by us and certainly unexpressed. Each of us had anger that we had learned as children to hide, so we were left with passive hostilities toward each other. Gradually, more and more, we "left" each other to take care of our individual selves in ways we had learned as children: Deb in her work and crafts projects and inhibited sexuality; and Mark in his eating, sexual fantasies, pornography, masturbation, staying up and getting up late, T.V., and general silence. Deb criticized Mark's lifestyle and Mark used her criticism to go deeper into his addictions and his silences.

During this time Mark became a diabetic, which he hated but which also became a source of nurturing. We sought help in a group of very fundamental Christian friends. We went to Bible studies and prayer meetings. Neither of us felt quite comfortable with this, but we didn't talk together, and it seemed like the "right" thing for a minister and his wife to be doing.

Mark pursued his lofty studies and Deb went off to her work supervising a dining service for one of the university dorms. Mark also preached as a supply pastor at local churches and received lots of affirmation for his abilities. While one part of Deb was proud of this, another part was resentful of the attention he got, and she found the grandiosity it seemed to create in him very difficult to live with.

Also during this time we gave in to having our first child, a girl. We were twenty-six and it seemed like the "natural" thing to do. While she was a joy, our lives became complicated by her needs, and we gave up opportunities to get caught up with studies, work, and survival.

Otherwise our aloneness from each other continued as did our lifestyles. Mark's sexual fantasies and masturbation graduated to occasional visits to massage parlors.

As Mark neared the completion of his Ph.D. he went to work as a pastoral counselor at a type of counseling clinic which had been pioneered by a father-type figure in the pastoral care field. We moved back to the city where our parents lived, and this placed us back in proximity to our dysfunctional families.

Mark found himself in over his head with counseling. He had been more academically than clinically trained, but he was expected to earn his own salary with counseling fees and was forced to learn by the seat of his pants. While he sought some supervision, his pride feared it. He had been raised to think that if you needed help you were an intellectual and personal failure.

Mark hated going to work, dreaded some of his counseling appointments and silently celebrated cancellations, but he could not talk about this with his supervisor. The center he worked for was constantly in financial crisis and he was underpaid. He finished his Ph.D., but was silently so unhappy he couldn't enjoy the accomplishment. It seemed to doom him to work he hated. Mark did manage to begin building a teaching and speaking career that took him away from home many nights. This was, of course, a convenient escape from the tensions at home.

Deb was home for the first time, at first without a second car. We purchased a home which financially strapped us, and again we fell into having a child, our first son. To save her sanity during this time, Deb began a business producing stained glass pieces, a skill that she had learned at the university. This business began to grow.

During this time we began exclusively seeing the couple who had set us up on our first date. The man seemed to have an exciting career as a lawyer and was fun to be around. He drank heavily, but while we may have noticed it, we never talked about it. Our children were the same ages and we became god-parents to each others' children. We talked in enmeshed and codependent ways of our affection for each other, even to the point of planning to move to a new place, perhaps even living in a communal house.

To this end we purchased land in another state, which continued our financial pressures. The man was continually pushing us to spend money on entertainment and other things like vacations together. Deb grew more and more uncomfortable with this, but we were enmeshed. Mark was really trapped in his need for approval from the man and went along with things the man did despite not really liking many of them. Often Deb felt left out of the social activities even though she may have been there.

As we vacationed together, we often stayed in the same room or cabin. On one occasion our enmeshment and flirtatiousness with each other led to sleeping with each other's partner. Mark remembers feeling that he "had" something that "belonged" to someone he so revered. Deb remembers feeling swept up in the event, not really approving, but not knowing what else to do. Mark's demands for sex, and Deb's encounters with his pornography, had already invited her into areas of sexual compliance which she found uncomfortable.

This episode destroyed our friendship with that couple for years. The man's jealousy of what had happened opened up sexual wounds in their relationship and they backed away from us. It has been only recently that we have done a Ninth Step with them as people we've harmed as a couple. This seemed to have a healing effect, but since they are not in recovery--he is still a practicing alcoholic, and their relationship is not good; we cannot move on to another level of friendship with them.

While we lived in this city, we also experienced pressures from our families. It was particularly hard to be with Mark's family, but we tolerated the pain of our discomfort. We attended Mark's dad's church, where Deb taught Sunday school. We went out to lunch after church. While Mark never was aware of this, the pain of his incest wounds forced Mark to do these things and, when doing them, to become silent and removed. They also fueled his addictions and coping strategies. Deb resented these "escapes," but again she had no tools to express her resentment in healthy ways.

During this time Mark became sexual with several of his female clients. It is clear that these episodes were about his sexual addiction, loneliness, and anger at what he was doing. They were also about his own incest and the boundaries that had been crossed with him.

Deb and those around him were oblivious to this. When an opportunity to go to a new counseling practice in a new city came up, it seemed like a good escape. To Mark it was an escape from families, from the other couple, and from the sexual relationships with clients. It was a geographic cure that would not work. To move, it seemed that we also had to sacrifice Deb's business, which was becoming more and more successful. Again we followed the pattern that what "seemed" good for Mark's career was the most important. The new job was for more money, status, and power: a bigger fish in a smaller pond (city).

In this new city we moved into a nice neighborhood, where those around us generally made more money than we did. We tried to keep up appearances; and we put ourselves in continuing financial binds. Mark was successful in his career, and Deb began to rebuild her business. She began to travel more on weekends. Mark's career made him very public in this smaller place. To test his own popularity he ran for and was elected to the local school board. Our third child, a son, was born soon after we moved.

Increasingly, both of us were away from home and from each other. We both had numerous distractions, the kids and our careers. At one point, right before our recovery started, Mark was counseling full-time, teaching college, pastoring a church on weekends, and serving on the school board. In these ways, we coped with the tensions at home. The angers and loneliness would occasionally surface, and we would have dramatic arguments. Mark would want to talk them through into the middle of the night. Deb would want to escape. Our sexual relationship was strained, infrequent, and full of dysfunction, but we were afraid to talk about it.

We went to see a counselor, but she could not help us as there were pieces of our addictions--mainly Mark's--that remained hidden from her. She was nice to talk to, and her role as a mediator helped for several days; but this passed and the tension returned. Both of us had thoughts of divorce and knew how lonely we were, and it was probably only our kids that kept us together during this time.

Mark's sexual patterns continued. A number of his work associates eventually did an intervention with him and he went into treatment.

Our recovery as a couple couldn't really start until recovery started for us individually. The main reason is that there were so many things hidden from each other (the "double life" that most addicts lead). Individual shame and addiction totally blocked any hope for intimate communication.

As Mark began to achieve sobriety, we also started to go to individual therapy, to men's and women's groups, and to a couples' group. In our first year of recovery we were gone most nights of the week to a meeting or a group. Our kids protested. Our first year was a time of painful honesty as long buried feelings gradually surfaced. Some of the anger took months to surface. The incest memories took nine to twelve months to surface. It was still a very tenuous time, and there were occasions when we still didn't know if we were going to make it.

As we experience the peace of the program, we find many things changing. We experience healing in all aspects of our relationship. We continue to struggle with the financial hole addiction carved out for us. Mark struggles to rebuild a career. Deb's business is very successful but creates enormous demands on her time. Although our primary addictions are in check, we can still distance from each other with work, moodiness, over-involvement in the kids' activities, and a host of other possible escapes. It is vitally important to maintain the discipline of the program. We find great strength and hope in each other, in other couples, and in the ability to share our story with others.

Mark and Deb L.'s Renewal

Let me love you without possessing you...

Let me share my feelings with you knowing you will handle them with care but not responsibility... Let me ask for my needs, knowing you can only sometimes fulfill them... Let my need for aloneness at times not be a rejection of you, but a time of nourishment for me...

Let me not depend on your affirmations of me, but live assuredly in the well-being of my own soul.

Let us be honest with each other...

Knowing we will not be ridiculed or threatened or ignored... Let us both find good friends without it being a threat to the life we share... Let us respond to each other without judgment or expectation, rejoicing in the moment to share intimately... Let us be weak sometimes or strong sometimes, knowing that both contribute to the growth of our relationship.

Let us dream together...

With the playfulness of a child... Let our love be a wellspring for the renewal of our own "little children," the safe place to nurture all of our feelings, the playground to experience God's abundant life.

Let us begin again today!

Deb L.

Mary and Dave B.

We were still in our thirties and still in our first marriages, which were not very fulfilling. At that time phrases such as "family-of-origin" and "dysfunctional relationship" had no meaning to us, nor would they for some time to come. We were both into our work, which we used as a means to isolate from each other.

Our relationship began with a chance meeting one evening at a local bar and restaurant. We were each with friends from work and we would deny that we were looking for someone that evening. But meet we did, and we followed it up with an agreement to have lunch the next day. There was no doubt in our minds that we were meant for each other, and the lunch led us to an affair that lasted the next five years. As a result we eventually divorced our partners and got married a few months later. We were full of optimism that this time we were going to do things right.

It was almost impossible for us to see what was really going on in our lives at that time. We were addict and co-addict fulfilling each other's needs and were blind to any reality. We would reshape our lives, and others would have to fit around our plans. It is interesting that our character defects were so invisible to us during this period. We were enmeshed. Looking back, we see there were plenty of warning signs about the problems ahead, but we were oblivious to them at the time.

A year after our marriage, our old behavior patterns began to surface, and the idyllic marriage began to develop "cracks." Dave had welcomed Mary's two daughters, saying that it would give him a chance to "do it right" this second time. Dave could see what he had missed with his own two daughters. Mary wanted a husband, not a father for her children. She wanted Dave to act like a friend or an "uncle" to them. He wanted to parent them with the discipline he had learned from his stepfather. It took another year for the marriage to get into really rough water; it became a destructive whirlpool that pulled everyone in.

Eventually we decided to seek counseling for step-parenting skills for the oldest girl, who was twelve and was starting to have problems of her own. Those sessions caused us to really look at our relationship and the reality it held for us.

Dave felt more out of control and confused than he could have imagined. The ideal life he had created was now coming apart. The feeling of abandonment was with him every moment. His job of some fourteen years was also in jeopardy as he had been neglecting it for some time. The "lie" he had lived with was out in the open. It was a relief, but it was also very frightening. Now he was ruled more than ever by feelings of shame and guilt and was heavily into his sexual addiction. His addiction continued the odyssey of craziness that affected the very core of our lives and the lives of those around us.

The fights, the rage, the isolation, the impotency devastated us. Dave's

67

other life was getting harder and harder to keep secret. Four years later the "Happily Ever After" marriage was virtually at an end. Dave tried to explain his sexual addiction to Jane, who went into a state of shock for a long time. She took it upon herself to learn everything there was about sexual addiction. The "watching" consumed her.

As he started reading the books of Dr. Pat Carnes, Dave admitted that he was addicted to sex. He promised to go to SAA meetings and did so for nine months. Then for the next four and one-half years he practiced a deeper secret that he hid from Mary. She was excluded from his secret life. Each felt that life was okay during that time. Mary didn't realize that Dave had gotten back into his addiction three years earlier. He clearly had under-estimated the power the addiction had over him.

There seemed to be no way to reestablish trust. The end, each agreed, had come, and they would part in a civilized manner. Now the secret was out with children and friends. Mary felt a great relief, even though the marriage had not made it. She proceeded with divorce despite feeling they really had some type of love. We both knew that the relationship would fail no matter what--or so we thought!

As Mary was waiting for the attorney, she picked up a copy of a national magazine and flipped through the pages, and there staring at her was an article on sexual addiction. It stated that whether male or female, sexual addiction could be treated successfully and the prognosis was excellent.

We met over the "last lunch." She explained what she had read, and Dave said he would find out more. His heart was finally talking. He found out that other couples were hoping to start a support group for couples in recovery. The necessary arrangements were made and we met with two other couples. This was the first RCA meeting.

The hardest part for Mary, however, had just begun. She started dealing with her responsibility in the relationship and discovered that she had brought many of her old traits, good and bad, into this relationship, as well as into her first relationship. In front of two other couples we made a six-month commitment to work on our relationship. We committed that we would not abandon each other during this time, no matter what (except for physical abuse).

Our major challenge was dealing with the underlying damage which was becoming so clear to us. This included lack of trust, couple shame, lack of intimacy, and a deep fear of abandonment. Mary was afraid of leaving Dave. She also was fearful of abandonment. We both realized we have a talent for zoning out. Now that the fear of abandonment was identified and spoken of openly, we could begin our work on our relationship and do some solid work in recovery as a couple.

Our weekly meeting helped us deal with so many crises, little and large. It was a safe place for us to open up to each other and to be honest in front of safe and caring couples. These two couples were instruments in our having a loving and gentle marriage. We thank them now and forever.

We cannot say that the hurtful words and actions are gone, but we can say we understand them and what brought us together. We realize all too well that it is an ongoing process. We still fight; however, the past hurts, mistrusts, and issues are in a clearer perspective.

Our mutual sadness about our childhood is now openly shared with each other. We understand that pain, but we do not dwell on it. We have lives to live and, most importantly, a true loving and intimate relationship to build.

Jack and Deb. M.

We have been married for four years and can say that we are really doing well as a couple for the first time. It has been a long and very painful road to where we are now, but it has been worth it.

We both come from alcoholic families. One is a survivor of incest (possibly both of us are), and both of us have had to endure the brutality of being raised in our out-of-control homes. We are in recovery for our individual addictions and attended the first RCA meeting in 1988. This is our story.

We met in the lobby of the apartment building where we both lived. Our first date was a boat trip on a popular lake in the Minneapolis area. We sat in a quiet bay and ate bread and cheese and talked. It seemed as if we could share for hours and never get tired of talking. We had an immediate "bond" and seemed to know what the other was thinking and feeling.

We continued to date each other, and the next few weeks we spent in each other's company most of the time. We talked until the wee hours of the night and hated to say good night and return to our apartments. We wrote love letters to each other and put "love messages" under each other's door. We were sure that we had found a "cosmic mate," someone who understood us like no one else could. Three months after our first date we were engaged, and eight months after that we were married.

All had gone well during the first few months of our courtship, as we were sure that we had found that once-in-a-lifetime partner. But, after we got engaged, the reality of what it might be like to spend the rest of our lives together became clear, and things started to change.

We began to doubt our ability to survive the mounting obstacles that arose as the wedding drew near. Could we reconcile our spiritual/religious differences? Would we handle a blended family situation with a child from a previous marriage? Would the pressure of our disapproving families get to us and tear us apart? Would the nine years' difference in our ages make it impossible for us to relate to each other? Were we making a mistake like our families kept saying? Following much pain, confusion, and deliberation, we decided to go through with the wedding.

After a small, private wedding (which none of our families attended), we moved to an apartment and set up house for the first time. What a shock! Neither of us was prepared for the feelings that were to come. Our sense of ourselves all but disappeared when we moved in together. We were unable to express our needs, both afraid of what might happen to our "perfect relationship" if we did.

Our blended family was the source of the most pain for us. Jack had a five-year-old son from a previous marriage, and Deb had no children. What at first appeared to be an issue of little concern quickly became the "Elephant in the Living Room." Deb had feelings of resentment toward Jack and his son because of the special relationship that they seemed to have, and often she felt "on the outside." Jack was aware of this and began to

70

distance himself from his son so Deb wouldn't leave him. Jack had a severe fear of abandonment. Deb tried harder to accept the relationship between Jack and his son. This brought about great feelings of resentment from both, and arguments became a regular occurrence.

As the weeks went by we stuffed more feelings and built more resentments toward each other. Our addictions were in high gear; we were both codependent, one bulimic/anorexic and the other a workaholic and relationship addict. We began to use food and alcohol more frequently, to numb our pain and resentments. Soon we were blaming each other for our misery and often talked of divorce.

We separated in the summer of 1988, unsure of our ability to make our marriage work. Our pain was immense, and no amount of talking, individual 12-Step meetings, or counseling seemed to help. The only thing which seemed to kill the pain was to not be together. We were truly on the brink of divorce.

Our higher power had a plan, unknown to us. We enrolled in a weekend retreat for dysfunctional couples called "We Came to Believe." This was the first retreat of its kind to be held and was an experiment of sorts. It showed us how to practice the 12 Steps as a couple and gave us tools to repair our broken relationship.

After the retreat was over, we knew we needed to continue the healing that had begun. Two other couples from that first retreat agreed to meet with us at a nearby church to talk about our issues as couples in recovery. We all felt a great sense of relief in talking with other couples who had the same kinds of problems we did. Our shame as a couple had been so great that we never talked with other couples about our problems. We had assumed that our inability to "be like other people" was a problem that no one else would understand.

That small church room was a haven for us. We were able to be honest in revealing our shame and powerlessness in our relationship and felt that someone understood what we were going through.

We are truly grateful to our higher power for our new life as a couple. We hope that other couples will find as much comfort and healing as we have.

MORE COUPLES' STORIES

Ann and Chuck

The Search for Intimacy and Commitment

Her Story

Chuck and I met on a blind date for a fraternity party. I was instantly attracted. I guess it was mutual, as we started dating.

I was in nursing school; Chuck was in college. He went home for summer break. I stayed and pined for a letter or a phone call, all to no avail. By the end of summer, I had finally given up any hope of hearing from him again, when a letter came a week or so before school was to start. I was instantly hooked once more.

Heavy drinking was an accepted part of the college scene in the '60's. Neither of us thought much about it. This was either naivete or denial.

We married and eventually had four children.

Over the years, there were times when I'd become angry about the drinking. After softball games, Chuck would stay out and come home fairly drunk. Friday evenings were "stop with the guys after work." Again it didn't seem too unusual, as all his friends did the same.

After twenty years of gradually more and more drinking and then lapsing into a maintenance mode, Chuck decided he was a problem drinker and was going to give up alcohol.

Abstinence seemed to be going fairly well. Like many others, I thought since he wasn't drinking any more, all our problems would be solved. Take away the alcohol and everything seemed just fine. Chuck undertook a new high-pressure job. Of course we hadn't heard about avoiding big changes during the first year of recovery. For that matter, we hadn't even heard of recovery!

Chuck's alcohol therapy group fell through. He was on Antabuse, but AA wasn't in the picture. His cravings weren't talked about. Day by day, depression started to creep in for him. But I didn't notice the slow decline in Chuck's energy or his low feelings.

In early January, now six months since his last drink, Chuck suddenly quit his four-month-old job. The next day his depression and suicidal thoughts were our main focus. We spent a terrifying day in the emergency room. The psychiatrist on duty felt it was inappropriate to treat Chuck because the psychiatrist had been and still was my own therapist at the time. We limped home. Chuck was put on anti-depressants.

We saw another therapist early the next week. She said unless we went to AA and Al-Anon, she couldn't treat us. It hadn't crossed our minds that his depression might be alcohol-related. We didn't know that 12-Step programs were necessary in our lives. Looking back, I feel the therapist was too hasty. She needed to talk to us once or twice more to help us acknowledge and accept the role alcohol had played and was insidiously still playing in our lives. At that time I was totally devastated: I felt I had reached out for help and it wasn't given. I was overwhelmed.

As a "good codependent," I stayed home and tried to do a suicide watch. I read about depression, noting the craziness in Chuck's frightening attitudes toward our youngest child, and toward life in general. I tried to control things and make them better-- "fix it." I had reached my bottom.

Finally, I just couldn't do it myself anymore. I phoned the hospital for the weekend therapist who was on call. Luckily, when I got through, I reached another therapist we had seen as a couple years earlier. I knew, liked, and respected her and her judgment.

I remember saying about AA and Al-Anon that we didn't want alcohol to be the focus of our lives. Wisely she asked, "What is the focus now?" Of course it was the alcoholic and alcohol, plus the resulting depression. A light went on for me.

I was getting emotionally more and more sick, being dragged down by my worry about Chuck. It was time to "Detach Lovingly," time to "Let go and let God." And I did it!

I went to Al-Anon and started taking care of myself. I learned more about alcohol, addiction, and codependency at a local treatment facility.

When my stomach was in knots, I'd go for a walk outside the house. I realized I couldn't control anything but myself and my attitudes. I learned not only "One Day at a Time," sometimes even that was too long--but one hour or even one minute at a time. This was pointed out to me by a true story on TV about a man sailing alone around the world.

Sometimes he had to break a day down into minutes or seconds not to give up. A month, six months, or a year into the future looked too bleak for me, but an hour or a day could be gotten through.

Meetings gave me support and encouragement, and of course a place to share my pain. I came away each time with hope, peace, love, and growth.

After about five months, Chuck decided he wanted to get better, too. An alcohol education and support group was available through our HMO. We started to attend together.

One of their premises, which I thoroughly agree with, is that the whole family is affected.

If one person is to recover, the family needs to recover, too. The alcoholic or addict and the codependent both need education and support about their roles in the dysfunction or disease. Recovery changes the couple dynamic. When one person is recovering, the other must change also, if they are to stay together and be happy together.

After "Family Night" we would go out for pizza or Chinese food with other couples from the HMO support group. This was one element of the fledgling start for RCA in our community. We could share with other couples who were working to change themselves in order to stay together.

73

In September of 1988, a 12-Step "Couples in Recovery" meeting was started in Berkeley, California. We debated about affiliating with Al-Anon or AA. Al-Anon was chosen in hopes of widening the group's appeal. There were just four of us at the first meeting, but the group soon outgrew our small room and moved to larger quarters in nearby Oakland. A second meeting was started.

Couples who survived active addiction and still felt there was good in their relationship were drawn to the meetings, as were couples struggling to recapture lost trust. Stories were told, and members shared how they dealt with painful issues from in-laws, to rearranging the household furniture, to buying a car together. Clean and sober couple friendships were started.

After the "Couples in Recovery" meeting had been growing in size for about nine months, a member shared about a new fellowship she had noticed in a recovery magazine. It was called Recovering Couples Anonymous. The California meeting contacted RCA headquarters in Minneapolis for information.

After much debate, our group decided to affiliate with RCA. It seemed to more closely address what we couples were looking for than did Al-Anon or AA. The Steps of RCA said just what we were hoping to attain: more commitment and more intimacy.

It's easier to share feelings and thoughts about couples' issues around addiction and recovery with someone who is gaining acceptance, understanding, and recovery from personal experience.

Even though each person has to put his or her primary program first in order to maintain health, the coupleship needs to be strengthened and nurtured too.

Our coupleship is stronger since sharing our experience, strength, and hope through RCA meetings. We value the love and friendship we have found in our recovering community. Each meeting is a reaffirmation of our commitment to each other and to growing healthier in a clean and sober relationship.

His Story

The support of RCA is warm and enriching. There's usually a special tone in RCA meetings, a vivid spirit of fellowship, sometimes a quality of awe.

Two years into recovery I started going to Couples meetings. Before these groups, I'd heard a lot of good advice and stories in other 12-Step programs but little about relationships, struggles with intimacy, sex in sobriety, and commitment to a partnership. I heard pained and angry complaining about members' partners, and for sure I was one of the blaming malcontents myself. Often it felt like "us versus them," and at other times as if relationship and commitment topics were bad form.

Ann and I, with our separate meetings, resented the other's "selfish" time apart. I know I'd grill her afterward about who had been at her meeting and what she had said or hadn't said.

I glowered about her going to fewer meetings than I did and also what I decreed were her less visible efforts and less driven resolve to work the program of my understanding(!). I identified with people in my own meetings and began to dis-identify with my partner. I started to feel "better than," superior, more informed, more aware.

Plus, with my long-standing fantasies of being rescued by females, I was especially drawn to certain program women; we would share long phone calls in the evenings, or strolls in the park, lunches, almost dates. Tension between Ann and me grew. Were our individual recoveries to take place in separation, and maybe generate even more strain between us?

Both of us felt this tension and sometimes were able to discuss it; Ann defensively and with hurt, it seemed, and me with haughtiness, badgering, and harsh anger. Looking back now, I believe we both sought more intimacy but feared greater closeness, both of us longing and resisting at the same time.

The Couples meetings helped right away. The group met first in a day-care nursery. (Today this seems highly appropriate!) We had been to Marriage Encounter years earlier, before our recovery had started. We remembered how we'd cherished the closeness we'd felt and declared we'd wanted. It was painful and distressing that this welcome connectedness didn't endure. In the Couples meetings, we felt others' awkwardness and defensiveness, longings and hurts. With hesitation, we started to talk of our own distress.

After a while, I was able to share about my sexual impotence during my great depression in early recovery, about my guilt in coming to the painful belief and understanding that while a practicing addict I had loved work and alcohol more than I did my partner, about my anger when we'd be driving through a ritzy neighborhood and Ann would exclaim, "Wow! Look at that big house!" I'd take this as a veiled, justified, and mean exposing of my deep secret inadequacy as a partner and provider.

Gradually I was able to share my confusion and bewilderment, groping to understand how I'd fallen into the months of extreme depression half a year after my last drink. Was it the collapse of a sobriety without a firm program? Was it my bottom around compulsive working and compulsive activity? Was it deflation and implosion, after years of growing rage and impotence being unable to control my partner, our finances, and our children?

Some of these things I'd been able to explore in my ACA support group, or in AA or Workaholics Anonymous meetings. But wasn't it dangerous and shaming to tell this in a Couples meeting, with Ann present? Wouldn't other couples take sides and judge me? Wasn't I inviting ridicule from members who could see falling-apart me next to detaching and accepting Ann? Wouldn't other couples turn to each other knowingly, and cluck their tongues and nod their heads, smirking as if to say, "Yes! Just as we thought! Another pretend husband! There *is* something phony and deranged about them!"

So my admission of powerlessness over our relationship was painful and difficult. And my group-level acceptance of that powerlessness was at first unimaginable. This despite having thought I'd done the First Step in three other programs.

I began to hear in other programs about practicing these principles in all my affairs, and began to hear members tell me of the progress they saw in me that I had not seen for myself, and later I started pinching myself and recognizing some changes, noticing my relief and diminished fears, the absence of panic attacks, night sweats, occasional dizziness in crowds, my initial alarm at being called on to talk in recovery meetings--all this good material, and then the jarring contrast of feeling like a critical, impatient, sarcastic, despotic, withholding ogre at home with my partner and kids. My sense of shame was scalding and acute.

Talking in meetings with one's partner right there adds a special dimension to relationship recovery, and also listening without interruption or crosstalk when my partner is sharing. Or noticing that another member has said something striking, and telling myself what a wonderful insight that person's just had, and what a beautiful gift I've just received to be able to make that insight my own — and later, to realize suddenly that in last month's meeting, or last week, or fifteen minutes ago, my partner had said the exact same thing, and I'd mentally rolled my eyes and had secretly wished she had said something more profound and riveting--"my partner, my spouse, who can make me and make us look good, or make us look bad", I'd tell myself.

As I write here, much of this sounds nasty, harsh, and unrecovered. And so it's a good reminder that lots of that has gone away, that I've been relieved of much of that automatic lashing-out and habitual contempt, the judging and loathing which served ever too well to keep my partner safely at a distance for ever so long.

For what RCA has helped me see was that my behaviors and thoughts, routinized and instinctive and promptly available as the rock-solid defenses they were, also kept me unable to get out of my self during those occasions when more closeness was desirable and safe, when deeper sharing without guardedness or fear of ridicule was urgent, when the yearning to break down "The Wall" was intense. I was starving at a banquet.

Now it's different during those institutionalized opportunities for painful stress and fear-generated hurtfulness like: April tax season, Christmas, in-law visits, or awkward dinner parties. Now we don't get nearly so crazy. When Ann does something less than perfectly (to my eye), I'm not as harshly quick to "clarify" her behavior for her or "offer helpful solutions" as to what she obviously should have done. All of that for me was poorly disguised abusive superiority to cover up feeling "less than" or excluded, or hurt about something I experienced long ago which my partner had nothing at all to do with. Thankfully, we're more able to accept weakness and vulnerability and confusion. We're healthier in conveying what we want from our pleasurable "couplings in recovery." We're more able to say "No!" with less fear of being withered in retaliation or igniting a two-week conflagration. We don't as frequently play master and slave, trading off occasionally for variety. As a couple, we're not so often paralyzed or angrily silent as before. Something amazing: we no longer have raging conflicts with our children or nasty fights about them.

A warmer and more loving relationship is actually being granted us. To paraphrase some program stuff, what we've received is a free gift, and yet in some small part we've made ourselves ready as a couple to receive this gift.

All of this helps a lot as I recover from two primary addictions, compulsive working and excessive activity plus alcoholism. In my recovery I get a lot of support from WA and AA, which in and of themselves are certainly a basis for a more joyous partnership. RCA helps me to be sober and more content in my two primary programs; the relief and hope I receive in RCA are an additional insurance policy for my recovery around work and drink.

So in a way, RCA is something other than my primary program, but it definitely is a glue or catalyst or strong supplement that serves to sustain my WA and AA recoveries. RCA helps me become available to receive some of the promises of the program. Other RCA members share the same thing in meetings.

Today I'm glad Ann and I are the couple we are. We're able to let go of many of our crazy-making expectations. It's easier to have and state our desires, hopes, and goals. For both of us, our fear is diminishing of being blind-sided by relapse or one of us recovering and leaving the other behind. Our tangible capacity for enjoying our lives has flourished.

Ann has inspired me through some of her changes, and also I've been grateful to see her lay down some of her burdens. Also, though and perhaps selfishly for me she's been able to be more there for me, and in being there, support me, to be me.

Our more intimate life together has supported me as I've sagged through dry drunks, or gotten crazy around jobs, or struggled with long stretches in recovery between jobs. One terribly upsetting event was when our sixteen-year-old son horribly broke his arm, a grotesque and nauseating sight, and all his awful suffering. Right afterward at the hospital, I had a strong clear vision that if he were put under general anesthesia he wouldn't come out of it. I'd had compelling visions and dreams before: I knew that it paid to heed the messages.

Well, I stonewalled the intake doctors, and the anesthesiologist. I insisted on a local anesthetic only, while we all waited for the other doctor who'd perform the five-hour surgery. I was grim in my determination not to sign the consent form. I resolved to protect my child by honoring the warning I'd received. You can imagine how Ann felt during all this!

The surgeon arrived. He explained why a local anesthetic just wouldn't

77

help. Gently he asked for our consent. Ann and I left to another room and I told her of my vision. Finally we decided anyway to give our consent. Ann was wonderful and supportive and considerate, but I'm so grateful that she was able to take full care of herself as well.

Chris was wheeled away. Perhaps it was one of those occasions when I really surrendered, not quit, just surrendered. Chris made it through the operation, plates and screws, gross incisions and general anesthesia and all. Soon I was able to accept that I'd been overtaken by normal terror, or perhaps that the outcome was different in a parallel universe or something. Ann and I were both able to be really there for Chris, for each other, for ourselves, and for our coupleship. Ann says she gets a kick now out of telling at meetings, "And Chuck was able to say afterward, 'Thank God it wasn't something to drink over!' "

Where are we now with RCA? We got a sponsor couple way back. We'll be doing our Fifth Step with them soon, so we're writing our Fourth Step now. We started two new RCA groups in the past sixteen months, and we go to two or three RCA meetings a week. Of course, we need our other programs as well. Ann is serving on the RCA Intergroup that's just been formed to support the five RCA recovery groups in our area and carry the message.

We've experienced a lot of our own euphoria in RCA meetings, plus the obvious excitement and hopefulness of most newcomers and regulars. In the last few months I've felt somewhat different in the meetings; maybe it's the end of the RCA pink cloud, or taking for granted the gift of the initial relief, or my stumbling around and in the Steps of RCA (how do you work the Steps as a couple??!!). Or the fact that there are no couples with twenty or ten or five years of RCA recovery we can look to and say, "There's what the future for us can be. They've got what we want."

Maybe it's the healthy release of an early illusion that Ann and I would finally, fully merge into one harmonious entity, no disagreements or disappointments, no drudge work left. Maybe it's a gradual withdrawal from codependency, while we grow and learn more about healthy interdependence, healthy caring between us. Maybe it's the Dreaded Fourth Step!

Today it feels more comfortable to be in a close, committed relationship with my partner, with our many different preferences and beliefs. The old habits die hard, but they are diminishing, little by little. Our wonderful times together are more common and less remarkable; while our average times together seem no longer mostly hollow or cold or distasteful and tense, lives of quiet desperation, but instead OK, pleasant, non-anxious. I don't feel "alone and lonely inside a relationship" anymore. No longer do I feel I could get healthier and better and get exactly what I wanted if only I were somewhere, anywhere, else.

In our meetings we've felt and seen our own progress and also the striking changes in others. Two couples who are friends of ours have gotten married in RCA. One pair has moved back in together. Two partnerships have had first babies. One couple got engaged. Some members have used RCA to help them reach the decision to separate or to end their relationship.

For myself, I'm grateful that these RCA meetings came into being. I no longer feel we're a defective couple or bad people trying to get good. The Fellowship has helped a troubled coupleship that longed to be healthier. Thanks, RCA!

Joy and David

A Fairy Tale

Once upon a time, there was a little girl named Joy and a little boy named David. Both of them came from families that were not quite like other families. When they grew up big enough to get away from home, they went off to college.

David and Joy met each other, fell in love and got married. They were going to have a wonderful marriage and for a while it was. They were very much in love and they were going to have a child of their own and have their own wonderful family. Things would be different in their own wonderful family, not like their childhoods.

But the evils of fortune struck them and the baby girl never breathed the air. They were both devastated. But David did not know how to grieve and he shut off all the feelings he could. Joy couldn't stop grieving and couldn't get help from David because he was shut down. Joy was put in a horrible hospital to make her stop grieving. David began to feel only through things that fed his ego, like sex and achievement.

They eventually had more children but that did not right the loss or regain the feelings. They pretended to have this wonderful, happy family, but they fought a lot about things that didn't seem to be as big as the fights. No matter how hard they tried, something was missing.

Now David could only get feelings through sex and work and he saw many other women to try to feel the feelings. Joy's feelings were mixed up. She wanted to believe that David loved her and the children. Just when she started to believe and think things were OK, David would be shut down and unavailable again. So, they separated from each other for two years and tried to figure things out alone.

Both of them were very lonely, David was mean and angry. Joy was sad and depressed and had to be both mother and father to their children. Each of them was determined to live as best they could. Then David found drugs and a whole new way to hide the real feelings and pretend to feel. Joy was angry that she was abandoned with two little children. She kept thinking that David would come to his senses and realize how much he loved her and their beautiful children.

After a while David and Joy began to live together again. But now David was high on drugs all the time and Joy was trying to figure out all his moods and there was no real intimacy or sharing.

Then David lost his job because he was either angry all the time or happy on drugs. So they moved to a big, fast, busy city where David found more drugs, more achievement and more women. David traveled a lot to other cities in his new job and he found women in these cities to try to make him feel better. But still there was no intimacy and Joy was still being mother and father to their children, even though David lived at home.

They were like two strangers in the same house. David's drug use got worse and Joy got help in Al-Anon. David was very angry when he was down and happy when he was high. When he was angry, he sometimes took it out by physically abusing Joy and the children. But one day Joy invited him to an AA meeting. After a while, he learned to live without drugs. But being in AA and NA and Al-Anon did not fix the lack of intimacy and communication between them.

David did not know it, but he became a love addict and he fell in love very easily with other women. Joy kept hoping that NA and AA and Al-Anon would somehow fix all the problems between them. Under the guise of detachment, she shut down to all the painful things between them. She thought that one more group, one more therapy session, or joining a church would make everything all right again. She hoped and waited and denied and triangled with work and kids and pretending and isolating.

David tried to stay out of other relationships, but he could not. He was a sex and love addict, but he didn't know it. He really loved Joy, but still there were only separation and blocks between them.

David tried to stay faithful, but he could not. And after he had nine years drug free, he began to sponsor a lady in NA. He really thought he could do that without falling in love, but he could not. He never should have been her sponsor. After a while he found that when he had no contact with his sponsee, he got depressed. He tried to stay away from her, but he was powerless.

Now Joy realized what was going on with this NA relationship and confronted David about the violation of the integrity of their marriage. David agreed to get help and entered SLAA. But Joy could not stop obsessing about David's sex and love addiction. She was very angry that David was throwing away their twenty-seven year marriage. She felt betrayed by David and betrayed by this woman who was associated with one of her work projects. Joy felt shame and depression and hopelessness. She went to COSA, but while she was obsessing, she lost her job.

So Joy went to a treatment center for co-sex and love addicts. David came to family week and they learned about their core beliefs. There, they found out about RCA and the "We Came To Believe" seminars. When Joy got out of the treatment center, it was close to Christmas time. Joy and David were so angry and shut down to each other that it took a meeting with both their sponsors to plan the Christmas season. They were both ready to call it quits and get a divorce. But they remembered what they learned about RCA, that "the only requirement for membership is a desire to be in a committed relationship."

David was sick and tired of hurting Joy and the children and Joy was sick and tired of being hurt. They decided to start an RCA meeting and found two other couples for the first RCA meeting in their area. A month later they went to their first "We Came To Believe" weekend.

A Reality Tale

Both Joy and David had a desire to be in a committed relationship. By using the tools of RCA which they learned in "We Came To Believe," they began recovery together. They learned about the baggage they each brought into their marriage and about how to recognize when they were "powerless."

They learned that David's father abandoned him with traveling jobs, controlled alcoholism and gambling. David never really had a healthy male role model. David's mother was dominating, controlling, arrogant, cold and matter-of-fact and did not show or honor feelings. She was not nurturing. David was often shamed in his family. He was never enough or as good as his brother.

Both of Joy's grandfathers died of alcoholism. Her mother was an abused ACOA who modeled the victim role, passivity, submission to anger, fear of authority figures, low self-worth, people pleasing, other-centeredness and toxic shame. ("I am not enough-I am somehow defective as a person.") Joy's father was an ACOA who brought abandonment issues (from his own father's alcoholism and death), controlling over-responsibility for others (he was the only one who could do anything "right" and "if something was worth doing at all, it was worth doing right"), perfectionism, authoritarianism, low self-worth, rage-aholism and toxic shame. ("I am defective and not enough.") Thus, Joy and David had a lot of heavy family-of-origin baggage to interfere with their fairy tale.

Joy and David learned about "coupleship" and how, as a couple, they were powerless over things which they used to blame on each other. They learned about making and taking time together in reflection and study. They learned to schedule time together. They learned about their Fourth Step as a couple and admitted it to God, to each other, and to another couple. They learned about dysfunctional intimacy and dependency and about healthy intimacy and dependency, and they learned about healthy conflict and how to fight fairly. Now they have a fighting contract and although they don't always use it, when they do, the real underlying core issues surface and can be dealt with, with understanding, compassion, validation and commitment. They took an Eighth Step listing the people they had harmed together and became willing, together, to make amends to them all.

Joy and David have learned that "living happily ever after" means living with presence in the today. They have learned that when they blame each other, that blame dynamic is really about each partner's core issues, baggage and wounded inner child. They can stop blaming and look at the real underlying issues. They have learned about the safety to feel and to express feelings. They have boundaries, express differences and negotiate comfortable compromise and agreement. They have learned to honor and respect each other. They are grateful to RCA and the spiritual awakening of their coupleship as a result of working the 12 Steps together.

Paul and Jane

Our Story

Our couple recovery began the day we walked into our first RCA meeting, March 4, 1990. At that point, we had been married for eighteen years with three children. We had each begun our own individual recoveries in 1987. However, our relationship was floundering, and we felt emotionally divorced. Even though we had been trying to use many tools from our own individual recovery programs, from counseling, and from other support groups such as Marriage Encounter, the way was not clear.

We had each made a limited commitment to try working on our relationship one day at time, but hope for couple recovery was scary. Pain and despair were frequent companions, and yet we also had many good memories of times together to use as sources of strength. We could each admit that important parts of our story had begun long ago in our families-of-origin. What we had not realized was the extent of the damage from our family histories, and its impact on our relationship.

What we know today is that couple recovery does work. As we share our story with you, we owe much to the support of many loving people in RCA who made it possible to share with you today as a couple.

Jane's Story

I'll never forget the night Paul came home from work and said he didn't know if he loved me anymore and wasn't sure he wanted to stay married. It was the day after a romantic weekend at a bed & breakfast, and I had planned a surprise fortieth birthday party with friends to coincide with our return. I thought we were really on our way to new growth, having begun our own individual recovery programs the previous year. My first reaction to his "bombshell" was to find a cure for my shock and pain-make love, go on a vacation, make a marriage enrichment weekend, anything to make the pain stop. The day before, I had given Paul a card that said, "Thanks for standing by me at this time in my life." I had no idea what was to lie ahead.

Through my 12-Step support groups (Adult Children of Alcoholics and Overeaters Anonymous), I had discovered that I used many illusions and defenses as protective walls to support a very fragile, lost, frightened and wounded inner child. My most powerful visual image of this child was a fallen little girl in the middle of an empty room with black menacing hallways surrounding her. This little child had surrendered, fallen, and could not pretend to be strong anymore. I was only just beginning exploring the depth of my emptiness. The frozen tears began to fall. How did the darkness begin?

As I was growing up in my family, long before I met Paul, patterns were developing which were filled with both healthy strengths and crippling

83

deficits. Today I am grateful for the peace I have found through recovery. I have given myself permission to feel all my feelings, and accept that my parents did the best they could with the tools they had available to them.

My childhood was marked by contradictions. When I was born as the fifth of six children in my family, dysfunction was clouding our family life. Loyalty, family fun, family rituals, spirituality, support and achievement were important values. However, alcoholism and codependency were also insidious poisons.

It was difficult and painful for me to relate to stories of alcoholism in my early recovery because my father stopped drinking when I was young. However, I'll never forget the two years he laid on the couch, believing, or so I was told, that he thought he had cancer. It didn't make sense. Here he was a successful doctor; why couldn't he go get help like he told other people to do. I was constantly seeking a bond with my father, to earn his love, praise, and recognition, but my brothers were his favorites. My bond with my father was incredibly important to me, especially due to my mother's emotional illness. My mother was caring, loving, and devoted. She was also a codependent, affected by manic depression, and an eating disorder. Her life was marked by a series of "nervous breakdowns;" the second of which occurred immediately after my birth. My mother was sent home to stay with my grandmother for several months. As an infant, I was cared for by my aunt, who worked full-time, an alcoholic maid, and my father, who had withdrawn into his own world of alcohol and depression. When I was eight, I was left at home to be her caregiver during a "breakdown." It would be thirty years before I talked about that day, and its horrible memories. That night, I crept out of the house, went to my aunt's down the street, and begged to go to school the next day. She charged over to the house and confronted my father, but the damage was done. I had broken the family rule of "Don't Talk". I'll never forget the look on my father's face.

We all had nicknames. I was so proud I was named "Princess," and I did my best to live up to it. I was always placed between my brothers in the car, and told to be the "peacemaker." Later in childhood, I was devastated when my father changed my nickname to "Chatterbox." During those years, the TV, the newspaper, and what my brothers did wrong were the frequent focal points for my father. I became increasingly angry and frustrated, but had great difficulty sharing these feelings with anyone. I could never understand how the TV was more important than me. I retreated with isolation into a safe world that I could control.

During my teenage years, the whole family was "bottoming out." I received no formal sex education, which left me naturally confused and naive. When I was sexually abused by a man on a public bus, I was terrified and hurt, but trapped by my lack of healthy emotional skills. Mostly, I got my needs met through academic achievement, creative outlets, and helping others.

I had learned from my family that it was not OK to talk about feelings, especially anger, fear, loneliness, sadness. Family messages that were powerful for me included: "Trust only yourself; If you want something done right, do it yourself; Put on a happy face; and, If something doesn't work out right, look the other way." One family member had said to me: "The absolute worst thing that could ever happen is to feel depressed. I will never, never allow myself to be depressed." I began to believe that I could control all my feelings. I also believed that I could manipulate any situation and make it better. Later in life as adults, I remember talking with my sisters about anger, and the difficulty we all experienced when sharing that feeling. I also remembered making a promise to myself as a child that I would never ever lose my temper, scream, demean, or be sarcastic with anyone. My anger felt like a firecracker with a burning fuse, waiting to explode. Although progress was made in the family, the scars went deep. An important healing occurred when my father shared with me that he could never take a drink again, since he was afraid that it would kill him and destroy the entire family.

At the end of my sophomore year in college, I met Paul. Our early days together were filled with constant conversation, fun, and feelings of belonging. I remember the solemn promise we made to each other that we would do things "differently," and not make the same mistakes our parents did. I felt important and special to him. What I overlooked was the fact that he rarely talked about his family or his feelings.

Paul's Story

Both of my parents are alcoholics and have been actively drinking since before I was born. They met at a "pub" in England during World War II. As it turned out, their meeting in a bar was to be prophetic, as alcoholism and the resulting consequences were to be a prominent theme for our entire family.

I am the oldest of six children, the "hero" of the family who always did everything right. On the surface I was the model child: good grades, never a behavior problem, well liked by friends and family. What my outward appearance betrayed was a lost child who had been emotionally abandoned at the age of fourteen months, when my sister was born to an overwhelmed mother who drank to forget her homesickness. Emotional trauma gave way to sexual trauma, as I was sexually abused by two teenage boys when I was four or five years old. I never dared tell my parents because "good boys" don't let things like that happen to them. The memories were buried for nearly forty years.

In grade school, I was quiet but studious. At home, the violent anger of my mother terrified me as I watched my brothers and sister run from her unpredictable attacks. My father was traveling all week and drinking all weekend. There was little help from relatives, although I did learn how to mix alcoholic drinks for my grandfather as I listened to his wonderful stories of World War I and early motor cars. Life was becoming more dangerous at home, so I learned to spend hours playing at a local park where a creek offered hours of solitude. It was here that I was sexually abused a second time by an older boy or teenager (memories are incomplete here). Even my sanctuaries were turning into war zones.

At the end of grade school, I began to consider entering a seminary to become a Catholic priest. At the time, I thought it was just another "wonderful" thing to do; as the Family Hero, I could make everyone very proud of my vocational choice. In retrospect, I was trying to get away from home as soon as possible in another effort to save my sanity. Get away from crazy parents and have salvation guaranteed. What a deal!

Just about the same time I entered the seminary, I also discovered that sex was a very powerful way to escape from my family and my own feelings. Pornographic books, "girlie" magazines, X-rated movies and erotic fantasy became my favorite diversions. There were dangers, of course, threats of damnation, burning in hell for all eternity, that sort of thing, but the power of sex for a fourteen-year-old makes hell sound like recess. I was hooked. For the next twenty-five years, obsessing, being compulsive, and feeling shamed around sex were to consume much of my available energy in life.

Our Coupleship

I (Paul) met Jane exactly five days after I had mustered the courage to leave the seminary at the end of my junior year of college. I make this point about the "five days after I left" because Jane would later defend herself in a teasing, yet fearful manner, lest someone accuse her of "stealing" a potential priest away from the Church. I had indeed left on my own to pursue "other interests" as I so formally indicated to the rector of the seminary. In truth, I had found out that leaving home didn't cure my spiritual and emotional hurts and sex couldn't fix them either. I had decided to try other people and the "R" word *relationships,* as the answer to the loneliness and depression that had marked my life for the first twenty-one years.

Jane and I met at a summer camp working with handicapped children. She first saw me performing in a small but fun rock band called the "Origin of the Species." I was drawn to her smile and her warm manner. She took my hand on a walk and I was in love. I hadn't been touched by a girl since playing Red Rover in third grade, but suddenly I knew what I had been missing during all those years of pre-celibacy: friendship, caring, fun, sharing with another person who cared, and closeness that was nurturing, not abusive. I had finally found a person I could trust.

Jane and I were married in 1971 and began our journey together. What we did well, we did very well. We played and had fun together. We talked, and created three beautiful children. We shared many common interests. We built on each other's strengths. However, our marriage began to unravel as the stresses of life crept in and the seeds planted in our families-of-origin

86

came to bloom.

I really had no idea about how to do a healthy marriage, since all I ever saw at home was my mom's anger, my dad's avoidance, more anger, more avoidance...an endless circle of futility tempered with liberal amounts of alcohol. At first I tried to be close to Jane, but all I really knew how to do was act like we were on a date have a good time, be together for a couple of hours, don't get too serious, and maybe have sex at the end. What I didn't understand was how to talk about feelings, how to ask for help, how to be supportive, how to argue in a healthy way, or how to talk about my needs. I had all of the responsibilities of a husband, and later a father, but none of the tools to do the job.

I began to distance myself from Jane as I felt increasingly trapped, lonely, bored, frustrated and scared about the future. As I began to withdraw, many of my old escapes from childhood and adolescence began to re-emerge. Fantasy consumed much of my waking moments. I returned to school and became absorbed in a master's degree. Sexual acting out with myself and other women became more frequent. I was on a downward spiral and heading for destruction. Fortunately for me, my Higher Power intervened by finding me a job as a consultant for a chemical dependency treatment center. Although I am not an alcoholic or drug addict, I am addicted to sex, fantasy, unhealthy relationships and intellectualizing. My addictions began to control my life.

The more I (Jane) tried to reach Paul, the more he withdrew. When Paul would try to reach me, I would be confused by what I saw as mixed messages. Our lovemaking had always been very special to me, and Paul made me feel important, unique, and special. As the years went by, though, I noticed that Paul seemed less interested. When I asked what we could do differently, he seemed confused and sad, but never really made any concrete suggestions. I often asked myself what was I doing wrong.

Despite our growing problems, the good times were always there, and our family life was very special. It was the contradictions that were bewildering. I would recoil from teasing and sarcasm or any form of anger, as I was playing out the scripts I had learned early in my life. Escapes were safe and frequent. Parenting, busyness, control, codependency, compulsive eating, and romantic fantasy novels were a big part of my coping. My bottom came at a time when we had a four-year-old daughter, we were both out of work, and I was eight months pregnant with a baby I was scared would have problems after the previous miscarriage. As my situation became more insane, so did my behavior. I began shoplifting. Fortunately, I was caught rather quickly, since it's hard to be sneaky when you are that pregnant. I really thought I had destroyed our marriage. Paul was surprisingly supportive, but still incredibly distant. I attributed it to my problems, graduate school and the loss of jobs. What I did not know at the time, and he didn't share, was that his behavior was just as insane as mine, since he was having an affair with another graduate student up until a week before our second baby was born.

A significant step in our growth occurred when we made a Marriage Encounter weekend. We joined an ongoing support group of other couples who were also encountered and began talking about feelings. That process opened the doors to deeper communication and sharing, but the addictions were still there.

Recovery

As I (Paul) began working in a recovery-oriented environment, I gradually became aware of how much pain I was in and the impact of my abuse history on my personal life. Most importantly, though, I learned how to begin my healing process through the 12-Steps and recovery fellowships where everyone wanted to be free from their individual, family and relationship pains. For the first time in my life, I began to feel some sense of hope instead of despair, peace instead of fear. However, my relationship with Jane was still confused and dark. I began to wonder what "love" was, and if I had any left for her. I chose to begin sharing my pain with Jane the day after my surprise fortieth birthday party. The black crepe was more fitting than my friends ever knew.

During the summer of 1988, Paul introduced me (Jane) to the 12 Steps of Alcoholics Anonymous. I had known about them intellectually, but never embraced them on a personal level. During the next year, I continued to focus on my individual recovery by entering a codependency treatment program.

I grew as a person, letting go of the old tapes that had been strangling me, stifling our relationship, and Paul. My family-of-origin and the healing of my inner child were the primary focus. Later, Paul told me that he thought about sharing his sexual addiction with me that same night after the birthday party when he talked about his confusion and despair about love and our relationship. However, it had been recommended that it would be helpful for him to look at his motivation and at Step Nine. I believe accidents do not happen in recovery and that our Higher Power was definitely with us each Step of the way. If he had shared everything then, our course of recovery might definitely have been different. The pain would have been more devastating, and my own individual recovery would have been severely challenged even more. As I grew in recovery, the imagery of the fallen child surrounded by dark menacing hallways gradually transformed into a garden of trees. The child began to blossom under the shining light of the sun, a powerful spiritual image of my Higher Power. The circle of trees at first were still very closed, and only gradually were other people allowed to enter safely.

As we developed separate recovery networks, however, our coupleship grew further apart. It was an incredible relief when I decided to surrender our relationship to my Higher Power and accepted my powerlessness to fix anything. But what then? How were we to work through the resentments, barriers, and broken trust? At this point in our journey, Paul shared the full story. Shock, despair, anger, rage, confusion, and depression were feelings that I now allowed myself to feel. There was also insight and understanding of the overwhelming degree of pain that Paul had been experiencing in his secret addictive lifestyle, and his history of abuse. Our First Step as a couple now began anew. I committed to staying in the relationship one day at a time, to share my feelings, but also to use other resources for support systems to work through my rage and my co-addict issues. We turned our relationship over to the care of our Higher Power. It would only be through a power greater than us that trust could be rebuilt.

Couple therapy did much to help us sort out our most painful issues, but it was through the fellowship of RCA that the shame and isolation of two abused and lost children would finally begin to be healed. We walked into our first RCA meeting filled with couple shame, questioning if there would be a future for us together. Gradually, Step by Step, our sharing of experience, strength, and hope with other couples helped our trust to be healed. Participation in the "We Came To Believe" program also did wonders for our shame and couple pain.

Together, we experienced a spiritual awakening that showed that the "Promises" were working, and that Step Two was happening. On a guided imagery, separate, but together, we each experienced our inner child meeting our partner's inner child at the same lake and on the same rock in Colorado. They took us to the adults, us, and hand-in-hand, we stood together, embracing all that life has to offer us in recovery with our Higher Power, and with you.

As a direct result of our couple recovery, we were able to recommit ourselves to each other on our twentieth wedding anniversary, August 7, 1991. What we know now is that we have the tools and the support to use as a couple as we face the many challenges ahead. We know it is safe to share with the many people in RCA fellowships across the nation, and that we share a common dream: to grow in our commitment, communication, and caring as a couple, one day at a time.

Gabrielle and Cheryl

When I (Gabrielle) met Cheryl, I was not looking for the big "R." I was involved with a variety of women at the time and so was Cheryl. We were open about our non-monogamy and comfortable with it. On top of that, I lived in Los Angeles and Cheryl lived in San Jose (about four hundred miles apart). I had no expectations of anything serious coming out of our relationship. After hundreds of dollars in phone calls and plane fares, I started to feel a twinge in my heart, and I promptly ignored it by dating someone new.

At the time, I'd been in many 12-Step programs for thirteen years and knew how to protect myself from harm, real and perceived. Cheryl respected my boundary of no chemical use while we were together, and smoked her cigarettes outside. I had no idea she had any addiction problems other than the obvious (nicotine), until she called me from a hospital to tell me she had been injured and a week later admitted she had a drinking problem. My first reaction was, "Oh no, I'm involved with a newcomer!" Apparently all the sharing I had done about how the steps and the fellowships had specifically helped me, opened the door to Cheryl's acceptance of the 12-Step approach for herself.

During this time I had been battling against an abusive supervisor at work and all the employees decided to walk out on the job in protest. This meant Cheryl was on injury leave for three months and I was unemployed. We spent most of that time together. We were no longer just lovers, we were becoming friends. The thing I liked about us was our cooperative tendencies. We traveled well together, with each helping the other with the mundane tasks. It was a real pleasure not to be competitive.

We noticed we were losing interest in dating other women. We both admitted we felt monogamous and freaked out for two days. When we finally calmed down we started to feel more comfortable in what was for both of us a new experience. Our only explanation for this strange occurrence was a Higher Power; it certainly didn't come from us. I think this was our first inkling that there was a Higher Power involved in our relationship.

The time was getting close for Cheryl to have to go back to work, and I had to start looking for work. Something in me (or something Higher) decided that I would never know if this relationship could go anywhere if we stayed in separate cities. I decided to move to San Jose. Thank the Goddess for the 12-Steps. I knew I needed to develop my own support network. I found my own place to live, looked for work, discovered my own meetings, and began to make my own friends. I really liked my independence and it felt good to know myself and to know how I wanted my life to be. The thirteen years in 12 Step programs had given me deep knowledge of myself and courage to go forward in my life. However, as soon as I moved to San Jose, Cheryl withdrew emotionally and sexually, and I panicked and raged. All my thirteen years of program went down the tubes. I had never worked the program to deal with being in and staying in a relationship before. I usually left when it hurt too much, believing it was them or a hopeless situation. This time a part of me said, "We are not leaving!" I felt trapped by my own inner conflict and raged at Cheryl, blaming her for my pain. We spiraled into a pit of awful arguments, painful feelings, and an inability to leave the relationship.

I interpreted her withdrawal as her wanting to leave me but not having the courage to leave. I felt I was invited into a big beautiful house and Cheryl ran into a room and shut the door in my face. I felt trapped inside and alone. This was my biggest nightmare, my core issue from my family-of-origin. I had the fear of abandonment and Cheryl had a fear of enmeshment; we were the perfect couple!

Gabrielle moved to San Jose the weekend before I (Cheryl) went back to work. I was just over two months clean and sober. To deal with my anxiety about returning to a stressful work environment, I put up my protective shield. I didn't recognize this behavior as shutting down; I was reacting to my fears the only way I knew how. With Gabrielle in the same city, I no longer had the cushion of miles to keep my distance. With daily contact, I was no longer able to disappear into my shell; I was in a monogamous (gasp), committed (gasp, gasp) relationship.

I was able to communicate with Gabrielle about physical aspects of life, but it was very difficult for me to talk about the emotional aspects. In my family I did not learn to express my feelings. All negative feelings (sadness, loneliness, frustration, anger), were either fixed or discounted. I learned to disengage from my feelings at an early age. Even when I could acknowledge a feeling, I did not have a vocabulary to describe it. My catch phrase seemed to be, "Hey, I'm a newcomer, I don't even know what a feeling is yet!" I was able to ask Gabrielle to point out to me when she felt I was withdrawing. I would then stop and examine what it felt like physically; it felt like my chest was in a blender. This was the only way I could learn when I was withdrawing. I also discovered that this was the feeling I drank over, smoked over, overate over, and was compulsive over. Through participation in the ACA program, I knew I needed professional help to assist me. I found a 12-Step therapist. Not long after, Gabrielle began to see the same therapist.

I (Gabrielle) didn't know about the hypnotic family state I get into when I'm vulnerable and intimate and sexual with someone. I always interpreted the discomfort as external factors. I had never thought that I invited my whole family into the relationship, or that I started to react to Cheryl as if she was my family. So by seeing the same therapist, I would have to begin owning my own projections. However, knowing this didn't stop me from going into my crazy thinking. I knew I was powerless over my interpretation of Cheryl's withdrawing, and still continued to rage and say crazy things that I later regretted saying. I felt like I was two separate people, and they didn't like each other.

Then one of our many miracles happened. I (Cheryl) read about

91

Recovering Couples Anonymous in a local recovery newspaper. We both jumped at the concept immediately. In the classified section of the same newspaper, I saw a notice for a Lesbian RCA meeting in San Francisco (fifty miles north of San Jose). We took this as a sure sign from our Higher Power. In the RCA meetings, we were amazed to hear that other couples experienced similar problems. We were not the only couple who had a complimentary dysfunction: where one partner's dysfunction triggered a diseased reaction in the other partner. When I withdrew, Gabrielle raged; when Gabrielle raged, I withdrew.

Cheryl worked on her tendency to withdraw and didn't always succeed. I (Gabrielle) worked on my tendency to rage, and didn't always succeed. I at first thought everything would be okay but I continued to rage. I got frustrated with myself and our continual participation in our complimentary dysfunction. It did get better and then we'd slip. Sometimes we didn't slip so far down. Sometimes, it was worse than ever. Cheryl finally got sick of me thinking she didn't want me. She told me she would release me from our monogamy. I knew then that she was sincere, and I believed that she did want to be in this relationship but she was powerless over her tendency to withdraw. I no longer took it personally. I began to see she was struggling with a lifelong pattern which started as a defense to help her survive her family-of-origin. This was a major breakthrough for me. This new way of perceiving Cheryl's withdrawal gave me new insights into Cheryl. I could see and feel her struggle and even feel compassion for her. I began to have the ability to let go of her withdrawal.

I discovered that instead of expressing what I was angry or upset about, I would store it up. I would obsess about it, interpret its meaning according to my way of seeing the world, and create a mass scenario in my head. It ended with me exploding into an insane rage. Cheryl, who was new to recovery, didn't know herself or how she felt well enough to know whether I was right or not. When she knew I was wrong, she wasn't able to articulate the correct interpretation.

We started to work the RCA program. We set up a Fair Fighting contract entitled "When We Funk Out..." Even though we didn't always follow the contract, it made us more and more aware of when we were in our couple disease. By acknowledging our communications breakdown, we discovered that some of it was due to our cultural differences (Australian English versus American English). But much of it was due to the different emotional languages of our families-of-origin. We found that we could occasionally stop the disease in mid-air. We found that if we said, "We're doing it again," we could create distance from the disease. What often helped was backtracking our arguments to find the exact point at which we began to react. Sometimes we were able to pinpoint what one said to trigger the other. We discovered that we have trigger words, phrases, tones in voices, and facial expressions. We gave each other permission to ask the other to rephrase something or to not use certain words. We then took time to find out what we meant by certain words. We gave each other the space to articulate what we really wanted to say. We no longer had to be perfect the first time around.

Cheryl came home from a CODA meeting one night excited about an RCA meeting in San Jose. It was wonderful having a local meeting. It didn't matter to us that we were the only gay couple there. In fact, it was amazing how much we identified with other couples regardless of sexual orientation. The first meeting that we attended was on the Second Step: perfect! We realized that our commitment and intimacy were in God's hands and not ours. Although our commitment was given to us (neither of us manipulated the other into it), we both did a dance around the intimacy issue. I felt Cheryl was actively running away from the intimacy, and I was trying (unconsciously) to control it with my rage. Knowing that the intimacy was in God's hands meant that all we had to do was work on the barriers that each of us put up against it. We learned more communication skills in RCA. We learned that it was okay to point out to each other what upset us about the other, as long as it was respectful, non-accusatory, and was said without directing anger at each other or intending to hurt each other. We also tried to explain why we were upset, "It pushed an old family button," for instance.

The other helpful aspect of the RCA program was discovering that we have a Higher Power looking over our relationship. We wrote a prayer which we recited every night before going to sleep. We've started to say the Serenity Prayer together every day, and before any discussions that may be trigger subjects for us. Reading the reflections got us talking about how we felt about various couples' issues. We began to acknowledge our Higher Power, and started to see where we've had Divine Intervention in our relationship several times already. We started to take walks, do outdoor activities, and experiment with new adventures together. We are coming to believe more and more in Our Higher Power. We sometimes feel as if our Guardian Angels are guiding us and our relationship. Other times it feels as if there is a cosmic force that visits both our hearts and joins us together. We sometimes feel that the universe sends special power to shoot into both our hearts when we are open and loving toward each other.

Despite the fact that our complimentary dysfunction wasn't yet eliminated, our commitment to each other deepened. We decided we were ready to live together. Moving in together triggered another level of my (Cheryl's) fear of intimacy. The first night in our new house we got into an argument. I felt I had recreated my family-of-origin and this confirmed my fear of intimacy, so I shut down even further. I felt totally enmeshed with Gabrielle because I interpreted her actions as if I were interacting with my enmeshed family. When Gabrielle would specifically ask for my attention, I would go into emotional overload and push her away. Gabrielle did not know I felt enmeshed with her. This triggered her abandonment issues. Our relationship was still on an emotional roller coaster. I felt I was at the end of my rope.

It was tough times for us both. It got so bad that I (Gabrielle) started to lash out at objects, like smashing a window and breaking furniture. I felt I was hitting a rock bottom around my rage. I started to feel my rage was not just about Cheryl, but was also becoming a channel through which I expressed all other angers, hurts, and fears. I had never wanted to become one of those people who was friendly to everyone and took everything out on their partner at home. Both of us independently were starting to doubt whether this relationship would make it. One night I gave myself permission to think about leaving the relationship. I cried for hours and went to bed exhausted and traumatized. The next day I woke up feeling great. I later realized that by feeling free to leave, I was free to stay.

Cheryl finally quit smoking, and I gave up my rage two weeks before our second Christmas together. What a miracle this has been for us. We disagree about this, but I feel I was able to give up the rage because she quit smoking and thus quit using nicotine to suppress her feelings. I find my life with Cheryl is so much easier when she expresses her feelings, even when she's grumpy. I am learning to hear her without interrupting her and without reacting to what she is saying before she is finished. Cheryl is learning not to instantly shut down when I do interrupt her. I know that when she expresses how she feels (even if I hate what she's telling me), it means she doesn't have to shut down or suppress her feelings. When she does occasionally shut down, I don't panic and go into my hypnotic abandonment issues. I'm amazed that I haven't raged, even though some of our problems still exist. We have been experiencing more intimacy and enjoying it.

I (Cheryl) no longer need to play the victim role, and I am discovering my many forms of codependence. I am learning to ask for space for myself (without feeling guilty). I am learning that I can be with myself even when I am in a relationship; I do not need to lose myself. I can take time away from the relationship, even if Gabrielle does not have other plans. I am developing an independent support network and learning to meditate with my Higher Power. By working my own programs, I am able to be present in the coupleship; by being present in the coupleship, I am able to grow in my own programs. This is the upward spiral our coupleship has been blessed with. I believe that being in this committed relationship has accelerated my growth in my individual recovery.

We have discussed doing a commitment ceremony, but we don't know how to include our families. My (Gabrielle's) parents hate the fact that I am a lesbian. When I'm single, they can live in the hope that I will meet a man and become heterosexual. So we don't usually talk about my sexual orientation. But being in a committed, monogamous relationship makes it impossible to ignore the fact that we are in a lesbian relationship. It is sad to think that the very people who should be my biggest cheerleaders at my marriage have such mixed feelings about it. I have a brother who supports me one hundred per cent, and an extended family my mother refuses to tell. I (Cheryl) have a large extended family and I am in a dilemma about what to do about wedding or ceremony invitations. My immediate family has grown to accept me and us, but it is still difficult to deal with what is traditionally a large family affair. It is difficult to decide whether to send out invitations with no explanation, or personally contact every aunt, uncle, cousin, second cousin, etc. to discuss my orientation with them individually. Am I setting myself up for rejection? How do I deal with this dilemma? This is one example of how gay relationships do have specifically unique issues.

To acknowledge and nurture ourselves as a lesbian couple, we recently started a lesbian RCA meeting. We have a standing joke at the meeting, from the Characteristics of Functional Couples: "We don't have to be socially acceptable." We still go to other RCA meetings because we have a lot in common with all recovering couples struggling to restore their relationship to commitment and intimacy. We attended the National Conference last year and had a wonderfully affirming time. When we arrived, we realized we were the only gay couple attending the conference. We wondered whether we should ignore it or say something in our introduction. We "came out" to break the ice in case people didn't know what to say or not to say to us. We were met with acceptance.

Our Higher Power keeps pushing us deeper into our commitment with each other. After several bad experiences around our rental house, we decided we wanted to buy a house together. This is now bringing up all our money issues. We have been able to discuss very difficult aspects without too much trauma. We believe it is because we are now better practiced at the communication tools we have learned through RCA. We listen to what the other has to say and not react. We check to see if we've heard correctly; then say what we have to say and the other checks to see if they heard correctly. We allow each other to have their feelings. When I (Gabrielle) react to Cheryl, I am distracting her from her feelings and injecting mine. When Cheryl is reacting to me, it disturbs my whole inner process and brings Cheryl into my focus instead of my feelings. We discovered this is a way enmeshment develops. Allowing each other to have our feelings is healthy individuation.

We have been in RCA and therapy for most of our two-year committed relationship. We have been through a lot together. Since I gave up the rage, I have slowly become more comfortable expressing my anger without fearing it will trigger my rage. I've actually found the opposite. The more I express my negative feelings at work, meetings, home, etc. the less likely it builds up into a rage. I can no longer fill up the rage sack with all the unexpressed feelings, and eliminate them all when I explode. I have to deal with all my feelings each day now that the trap door to raging has been removed. I have become more real. Cheryl says it is like being with an entirely new person. I am no longer afraid that Cheryl wants to leave me. I am more able to let Cheryl be Cheryl and truly observe, discover and appreciate her for who she is. I (Cheryl) feel safer to come out of my shell. I am more trusting that the other shoe is not going to drop. I am more confident in my feelings and am able to express them without fear of ridicule or shame. I am feeling freer to express my sense of humor.

Being two separate human beings feels liberating. Being intimate feels liberating too - we are free to love.

We have to keep remembering we have a Higher Power taking care of our relationship. Nothing bad is going to happen just because we are having feelings about something, or disagree about something, or have a seemingly unresolvable problem. There is nothing that can hurt our relationship if we are working our own and the RCA programs to take care of business, and allow Divine Intervention to take care of the impossible.

Pat and Gene

Pat's Family

Pat came from a large family of nine children. Her dad owned his own business and was a chronic alcoholic until he died at age fifty-two. Since Pat was second oldest, she had become a good caretaker, not only of brothers and sisters, but of her dad, too. Dad could only have emotions while drunk, which was daily. Pat's mom would leave nightly to escape confrontations with her drunken husband, who was physically abusive with one of his two sons. Pat's parents had a very passive-aggressive relationship, which the children learned along with blame, dishonesty, denial and hopelessness.

At age seventeen, Pat's mom kicked her out of the house in anger one night when Pat hadn't done all the dishes. Pat decided to move in with her sister. A year later she went to Europe for two years while her parents separated. Her dad went to a halfway house. Pat was always in the middle of her parents' marriage. The night her dad died, she was at the hospital with her mom, whom Pat had called to come.

"Why?" they each asked her privately.

"Because you love each other," she said. No one had told her they didn't or that it was not her job to keep them together. (This triangle pattern has been an important issue for Pat in her recovery.)

Pat spent the next five years working on her individual recovery in 12 Step programs while also attending the University of Minnesota.

Gene's Family

Gene's dad was a survivor of the Holocaust. Only a few family members lived to tell about it, although things were kept pretty secretive. His dad turned against God in anger over this tragedy and became an atheist/agnostic. His dad's profession took Gene's family all over the world. They moved on a regular basis.

Gene's mom was emotionally and physically abusive to him from the age of three. His dad was not present much, either physically or emotionally.

Gene became chemically dependent in his early teens and was capable of violence in his disease. After eight years of destructive behavior, Gene finally entered detox and began his recovery. Gene's family (one sister) chose not to participate or support him in his recovery. There was also a hopeless theme in his family.

Gene and Pat had some parallel experiences: each had come from a dysfunctional family; each had been in their individual recovery for five years; neither had been in a serious relationship since they'd moved out from their significant others, five years earlier. They were ready to give things a try between themselves.

Because they attended a support group together, they quickly became

97

aware of some of the issues they had as a couple. Anger was a major problem. Although Pat was attracted to the way Gene could express his anger so easily, it soon became difficult for both of them when she expressed hers. Gene was attracted to Pat's ability to express her other feelings, except when she got angry; then he would shut down completely.

Something was feeling very familiar. They were reliving their parents' relationships of rage and emotional withdrawal. Both of them felt trapped and neither of them knew how to break the cycle that seemed to overwhelm them. Pat was into smoking and food addiction and could not figure out what was wrong even though she and Gene were in counseling on and off for several years.

Since things didn't seem to be getting better, Pat thought being a mother would help fulfill her needs. Getting pregnant was a power struggle. In fact, life for Pat and Gene was one power struggle after another for a long time. They were both good reactors.

In five years, Pat and Gene had gotten married, had two babies (major surgery), bought a house, maintained their jobs, and attended individual recovery programs as well as kept up friendships. Life was busy and their focus was on the external rather than on their marriage.

They hit bottom the year following their second child's birth. Either they wouldn't talk to each other at all, or there was lots of sarcasm. Pat had quit smoking before getting pregnant but was just beginning to deal with her food addiction. As the months went by they were spending less time together and becoming more distant. They finally ended up in separate bedrooms.

The tension level was always high; there was no laughter; no time for family activities and no peace. The screaming and shouting got out of control. They quit their long-time therapist and saw a crisis counselor, who helped mediate all the anger. By this time Pat, was in a 12-Step program for her food addiction. They continued seeing this counselor for a year. Then Pat realized that this counselor could not hear her when she got underneath the anger to the other emotions. Gene was ready to leave.

Pat and Gene had left therapy for four months and still felt stuck. Neither one was interested in further therapy. They had learned about a couples' 12-Step group a few years before. They went one night while Gene was on vacation just to check it out. That was their first RCA meeting. Immediately, they felt at home, they were terrified of what would happen yet knowing they too belonged.

Things have changed a lot since that first meeting. They have realized how difficult it was to try to resolve some of Pat's "triangle issues" because the therapists re-activated the pattern in an unhealthy way.

It has been a gift to have other couples be so honest and share their struggles with us. We have been much more respectful of each other and can let go of our "unresolvable issues," knowing that God is with us. Even though both of us had been in individual recovery programs for fifteen years, we had not learned to "let go and let God" as a couple. It was a big step to release ourselves from the blame and the need to have all the answers.

Now we can bring our strength and experience to the group and support others like ourselves. The shame is still there at times, but we can release it and heal from the past. "You will know a new freedom...;" "Keep coming back; it's working..." Things may not be perfect, but we're learning to accept ourselves for who we are, individually and as a couple.

Beth and Stephen

Freedom From Bondage

Beth's Story

I am thirty-two years old, and have been in relationship with Stephen for three years. We have been attending RCA meetings together steadily for a year and one-half. Prior to meeting Stephen, I was sober in Alcoholics Anonymous for almost three years. God willing, I will soon celebrate six continuous years of sobriety in that program. Little did I know when I first got sober what other addictions awaited my discovery and my recovery from them!

I was the first of three children born to a couple who were, in my not so humble estimation, already deeply engaged in their own addictions. My mother, in my opinion, was addicted to rage and to my father; my father to alcohol, gambling, work, my mother, and enmeshment with his mother. I believe that my mother was emotionally abused by her parents from early childhood. I recall her frequently saying that she didn't feel free until her father's death. Sarcasm and name-calling were the operative means of communication in her family, and those patterns were repeated in my family. My brother was referred to consistently by his full name, with his middle name replaced by either "liar" or "whiner." Raging and screaming, including the following routine phrases, were directed at us morning, noon, and night: "Get out of my sight; I'm going to rip every g--damn hair out of your head; I'm going to brain you; I'm going to shove my fist down your throat; I'm going to break every bone in your body; I'll give you something to cry about." My mother prided herself on having a repertoire of dirty looks, of the "if looks could kill" variety. These looks were not used to ensure we minded our manners in public; i.e., as a replacement for humiliating public reprimands. They were an integral part of the family communication system, as were my father's silences, which could go on for weeks or months. I learned all of these behaviors, and until sobriety, thought that practicing them was the normal way to have a relationship. Learning new ways of communication has been absolutely necessary for me, in order that I might have any chance at intimacy.

My father was one of two boys who were "mommy's little angels." During my childhood, I observed my father and his brother being continually invaded emotionally by their mother. I presume this invasiveness began in their childhood, and that, in response to this invasiveness, my father learned withdrawal and silence as a defense. He used "the silent treatment" as a form of punishment against my mother, and later, against us. This was the way he expressed his hurt and anger, and I learned to do the same. He also learned, in his family-of-origin, that children were for the use of adults, not that adults were responsible to meet the basic emotional needs of children.

100

In both my mother's and my father's families, the children were made responsible for the parents' happiness, and this turn-around of parent/child roles was repeated in my family. My parents did not take emotional responsibility for parenting us. Instead, we were required to provide for their emotional needs. It was our job to receive their rage when it overwhelmed them, to stop our tears in order not to make them uncomfortable, and to cuddle with them when they felt the need for loving, not when we needed such attention. My two brothers and I were also made responsible for our grandparents' happiness, especially after both our grandfathers died and our grandmothers were left without partners.

As part of being responsible for our parents' emotional needs, we had to play assigned roles, and, insanely, were then shamed for doing so. This took the focus off our parents' misbehavior. I was the "smart one" with the "big mouth," and my brother was the "not so smart" one who "lied" all the time. Of course, I lied too, but they did not confront me with it in order to preserve their assigned family structure. My littlest brother was the "good" one. Interestingly, we were assigned our roles before we really had the opportunity to develop our own personalities, and the roles we were assigned closely paralleled our same-sex parent's particular dysfunctions. For example, I was known as cold, sarcastic, and unemotional, with a repertoire of dirty looks. These characteristics were my mother's, the result of her childhood abuse. My brother was cast as "not so smart," which is the role my father played, both to avoid parenting responsibility, and as part of his addict dance with my mother. She was the "smart" one, and patronized him, while he wielded his power under the table through the threat of silence and withdrawal.

Silence was also an integral part of the family communication system, in a different way than simply as my father's punishment of us. We had to be silent about what was happening to us. I eventually became so silent about what was happening to me that I stopped knowing what was happening to me. This created my current difficulty trusting, or even being aware of, my own perceptions. I am working to overcome the resulting hypervigilance, and over-dependence on "rules" to determine how things "should" be, as opposed to how I feel. I am learning to feel my own feelings and to trust my own judgment, so I can stop constantly evaluating my behavior and that of others, especially Stephen's. This does not mean, of course, that by ceasing my endless intellectual evaluation, I wish to avoid the Tenth Step, or that my goal in using my own judgement is to allow self-will to run riot. What I am striving for is balance, here, as in all areas of my life.

The requirement for silence also created immense shame in me. One way they enforced the silence was to shame me and call me names (argumentative, oppositional, etc.) whenever I disagreed with their assessment of me. I am not speaking here about the type of shame one appropriately feels when one has offended or done something unacceptable. I refer to deep, pathological shame; the sort that makes you feel like you are defective at your core,

101

that you are disgusting even for existing and drawing in breath. I came to believe it when I was told that I was crazy. Since nothing was wrong with my parents, something must be wrong with me. I am healing this shame, one day at a time, and it is only by healing this shame that learning new ways of communication is possible. I realize I cannot impose a veneer of "appropriate" communication over a shame-filled spirit. I understand why my parents behaved as they did, and believe that they are shame-based as well, and could only give me what they had inside themselves.

My father gave up gambling when he lost a $40,000 loan by gambling it away in the stock market. He learned his drinking and gambling behaviors at his mother's knee. His parents owned a tavern, and one of my earliest memories of my grandmother was the recollection of the enjoyment she took from going to the "track," i.e., to the horse races. After giving up gambling, my father began to rely more heavily on his drinking to sustain him.

Physical abuse was present in my family, which leads me to believe that my parents experienced similar abuse as children. Both my brother and I were routinely beaten for simply doing what children do, crying, saying "no" when we were toddlers, etc.) Although I am fiercely opposed to spanking a child of any age, for those of you who are not, I will distinguish here between my understanding of beating and spanking. Spanking, in my view, is a non-painful blow delivered with an open hand, on a well-diapered toddler bottom, by a calm parent, for the purpose of teaching. Spanking never involves the use of objects (belts, hairbrushes, etc.) to deliver blows, and never involves repeated blows. Beating is the delivery of blows to a child by parents who are in the midst of their own rage. My brother and I were beaten. I don't say "brothers," although I had two, because I have many gaps in my memory, and I don't remember what happened to my youngest brother regarding beatings. I remember feeling that my parents had let up to some degree in their treatment of my youngest brother, but I truthfully do not recall. I left home when he was six and I was sixteen.

I never knew what behavior on my part would "cause" a beating, and what would merit praise. Throughout my childhood, I had a recurring nightmare. In this dream, an unspeakable, invisible evil would be chasing me through our neighborhood. I would manage to escape into our house, and I would feel deeply relieved to have made it to the safety of the kitchen, where my mother was standing, back toward me, stirring a pot on the stove. I would begin to describe my desperate flight, and my miraculous escape. My mother would slowly turn around to face me. As she turned, I would see that her face had turned to wood, much like that of a wooden ventriloquist's dummy. She was possessed by the invisible evil that had pursued me. I would run screaming from the house to our neighbor's home, where the same thing would happen again. I had this dream repeatedly through my childhood, and sporadically into my adulthood, until I got sober. Once I realized that the dream was a true description of my life in my family-of-origin, I never had the dream again.

Sexual abuse was also part of my family-of-origin experience. As a toddler, I had a bladder infection for seven months, which only stopped after I was hospitalized for two days for diagnostic tests. The doctor's notations each month referred to genital redness and irritation, but no one intervened. The tests did not cure me, and the doctor did discover that there was no congenital abnormality causing the problem. Apparently, the hospitalization scared whoever was molesting me enough to make them stop. In addition to my early experience, I was also abused by my paternal grandmother. After the death of her husband, she would sometimes whine, "Make a little love to me," and then I knew I was in for it. She did not mean intercourse, but meant that we were supposed to meet her needs for physical touch, which were sometimes sexual. I was also forced to sleep with her, both when I would visit her apartment, and in a trundle bed in my bedroom when she stayed over on weekends. This was a set-up for my own abuse. She frequently sexually abused my youngest brother in front of me on the family room couch, in the guise of comforting him. This was both disgusting and exciting to me at the time. It was both relieving and painful, in that I was greatly relieved to no longer be the focus of her attentions, but I felt abandoned and jealous as well.

Emotional sexual abuse also went on in my family, in many forms, including comments made frequently about my developing breasts, and a rivalry developed between me and my mother regarding the fact that my breasts were much larger than hers. My parents expressly taught me (not just in messages and by example, but in words) that I came second to their relationship with each other. They explained that children always grow up and leave their parents, so children come second. Someone would come along and love me one day, they explained, and then I would be first to that person. But until then, I had to wait. I learned sex/relationship addiction early on from what I was taught in my family-of-origin, both by example and explanation. Sex was love, as I clearly saw, both by the fact that the only touching I got that wasn't beating was from my grandmother, and from the way I saw my mother behave with my father. I got the clear impression that men were incredibly stupid and easily manipulated by sex, but also, somehow, incredibly necessary. I knew, in my child's understanding, that to be loved as an adult, you had to read the book in my mother's drawer about "how to please a man," because if you didn't, they would leave you, and then you would die.

It was with these lessons that I was armed to face the world when I left home at sixteen. I had become sexually active at age fourteen with my high school boyfriend, who I later realized (in my sobriety) was an alcoholic. He drank prescription codeine cough medicine out of the bottle when he didn't have a cough...I always wondered why he didn't use a spoon, and why he took it in the absence of a cough! He went to college and broke up with me. I was devastated. I went to the same college he did, even though it was out of state, in hopes of getting him back. Immediately upon arriving, I began using drugs and alcohol. When my youngest brother was diagnosed with leukemia, I increased my drug use to daily use. I did hallucinogenic drugs during the week I gave him a bone marrow transplant, although good girl that I still was, I checked with the doctor first. When he died, I was expected to comfort my parents over the loss of their son. As they had learned that children were to serve the emotional needs of parents, it never even occurred to them that they were responsible to parent me through the loss of my brother.

At college, I fell into the arms of a man whom I disliked the minute we met. I ignored my first impression, which was that he was somehow oily and dishonest. Although he began cheating on me within four months of the initiation of our relationship, I stayed with him for nine years. He was the one who would finally love me first, in my addicted mind. He was educated and articulate, interested in public affairs, and compassionate. Of course, he came from an abusive family too, and learned techniques of communication from them, so his sweeter spirit was increasingly masked as his disease progressed. His family was very kind to me, and this also kept me with him. They welcomed me for two weeks at Christmas every year, and they took me on long family vacations to the lake every summer. Although his father used name-calling and raging too, since I was not a family member, it was not directed at me, and I felt safe in their home. My parents had long since stopped taking me on family vacations, saying they didn't like me. So being welcomed by his family was like heaven to me, until the end, when I started learning about alcoholism and dysfunction.

Initially, my partner and I used together; more and more our addictions drove us apart. He drank and was abusive, occasionally physically; I used and was abusive, relying on my old standbys of name-calling and raging. He threw me across the room in January of 1985. The first time of the few times he hit me, my mother said that I was so difficult to live with that I probably provoked him, and I should just try harder to be nice. I was angry, but I believed her, and stayed for another eight years. This time, somehow, I knew we needed help. We went to counseling, and the doctor said we needed individual help. Since I was afraid that my partner would not go back to therapy if he was forced to change therapists, I found a different counselor for myself. She immediately required me to go to Al-Anon as a condition of seeing me. So, I went.

Within three months, he quit therapy and hid the fact from me. I found out and, after two months of hoping he would get another therapist as he promised, asked that we separate. Not yet in recovery from my relationship addiction, I only got the strength to ask him to leave because I was carrying on an intrigue with another active alcoholic with whom I worked. I "knew" I wouldn't take the relationship further, but when this new fellow got sober the week my partner left, I became involved with him. When, after several weeks, the grief hit over my partner's departure, I attempted to break off with the new fellow and go back to my partner, but he was already involved with a young girl. We went back and forth, until I collapsed and went into treatment for codependence. I had a dream there that I was an addict, and that if I admitted it, I would feel better. When I told the dream to the group, instead of laughing and saying, "Oh, pshaw," much to my disbelief, they all shook their heads in agreement!

I came back home, got involved with the guy newly sober in AA, got sober myself, and lived happily ever after in relationship addiction until I discovered his sex addiction. Then, it was back into the fetal position for me. I got into ACA recovery. After a lovely year on my own, in which I learned, deep in my gut, that God was enough for me, and I was enough for me, I met Stephen. I was at a meeting where I was a regular, and I noticed him because he was a newcomer to that meeting. He shared about doing body work in therapy, which was one of the few forms of therapy I respected. I was intrigued. Then he began to talk about what he was doing in that day's therapy session, which was dealing with the fact that he did not want to have sex with the woman he was dating. I thought this was great! A man who also did not want to have sex sometimes; a man who felt like me. He came up to me after the meeting to chat, and he was so soft-spoken and nice. My friend Allison was standing with me, and after he left, she said she hoped he would stop dating the woman he referred to in the meeting, and start dating me, because she thought he seemed so nice. So, after the meeting the following week, we went out for coffee. I then realized that he was active in his sex/relationship addiction, and he wasn't just dating the other woman casually, he was living with her! I "knew" I wasn't going to get involved with him! Ha! Two weeks after we met, he left his relationship and started to go to SLAA. I went for it!

Getting involved with Stephen, even against my better judgement, was the clue to me that I was a sex/relationship addict. In my relationship with my partner of nine years, I thought the problem was his alcoholism, when, in fact, his alcoholism was a mirror for my own. With my first partner in sobriety, I thought the problem was his sex addiction, which, in great part, it was. But when I got involved with another sex addict, which I vowed I would not do, I realized the lesson was the same and admitted my powerlessness over my sex/relationship addiction. Initially, I liked to keep a safe intellectual distance from the "sex addict" stuff, and just say I was a relationship addict. I never did any of that disgusting promiscuity stuff, or used pornography, or...but, when I heard myself listing all these items in my mind, I heard the "not-yets" of AA and remembered what denial sounds like.

Slowly, just as in my alcoholic sobriety, I have remembered things I did, and thoughts I have, that put me squarely in the sex addict class. I now realize that there is no difference between sex and relationship addiction. Just as in AA, some people drank beer, some fine wine; some were in the gutter, some were in the corporate board room; some had a D.W.I.; some didn't. So it is in SLAA; some were prostitutes, some were housewives; some used pornography, some just used seductive clothing and flirtatious behavior as their stock in trade. But just as we all in AA are alcoholic, whatever floor of the elevator we got off on, I cannot put myself above those disgusting sex addicts whose behavior I hold in such contempt. I am one. Of course, I still struggle with my contempt, and my desire to separate myself, but God provides me with plenty of reminders that whenever I have one finger pointing away from myself, I have three pointing back at me.

In spite of our addictive start, the fact that I was attracted to Stephen was a sign of my healing. He had six and one-half years of sobriety in AA when we met. This was a definite improvement over the active alcoholics I had begun relationships with before. He was already in therapy for himself, not because anyone was making him go. Also, because of my physical abuse, I had previously only sought relationships with men who were very slightly built, and not too tall, as I thought that somehow this would protect me from abuse. (Wrong!) I was also turned off by any obvious indications of masculinity, dating only men who were hairless and as close to womanly as I could find. Stephen, on the other hand, is six feet tall, very muscular and hirsute, and unmistakably male. Trusting in our commitment to non-violence with each other was a big step for me, as he is certainly large enough and powerful enough that he could kill me if he wanted to do so.

Many of the experiences I had, and behaviors I learned in my family, affect my ability to participate in an intimate relationship today. While my problems started there, my healing and changing are my responsibility. As a child, I was a victim, and so I learned to be both victim and abuser. I cannot blame my parents, or somehow separate myself from "child-abusers," and consider myself superior. I am as they are, and I can only be grateful that I have been given the opportunity to change my behavior and to break the abuse chain. My "automatic pilot" behaviors, when active, are things that damage my relationship and are problems Stephen and I have to deal with in our healing together as a couple. My propensity for violence; screaming and raging; name calling; my post-traumatic stress disorder, which causes my "fight or flight" response to be permanently stuck in the "on" position; and my related constant anxiety, hypervigilance, and inability to relax are all things I am working on changing with the help of RCA and other 12-Step programs, therapy and body work.

Regardless of our awareness of our family issues, I find that we act out aspects of both our parents' addict dances, and even mimic some of their circumstances. I guess the Big Book is right when it says self-knowledge availed us nothing! Some of the similarities are astounding. I have an advanced degree; my mother went to a prestigious university. Stephen and my father completed high school and did not go on to college. I patronize Stephen; my mother patronized my father. Both my mother and Stephen's mother raged; I rage at Stephen. I often struggle with the contempt for men I learned growing up in a family where the role for all the men was "stupid." I am overly responsible; Stephen uses under-responsibility as a way to withdraw, which often draws my contempt and rage, and relieves him of his responsibility to deal with his own anger, just like my father. Stephen's defense mechanisms against his invasive mother include withdrawal, which he uses in our relationship as my father used with my mother and me. Stephen also uses crazy-making, table-turning, and subject-changing as addictive fighting tools, which parallel the crazy-making that was non-stop in my family-of-origin. The good news is that, thanks to the Steps, and lots of help, we can see our patterns, which, while not enough in itself, opens the door to healing them.

Stephen's Story

I am a multiply addicted person. My addictions and compulsiveness are full-blown diseases, yet, as paraphrased from the AA Big Book, they are but symptoms of deeper underlying causes. More concisely, I believe these addictions to be coping mechanisms that I adopted as a child to alleviate emotional stress. The causes of my childhood stress are numerous: ineffective or absent emotional and social skills, incidents of abuse or trauma, and so on; however, the greatest underlying source is the parenting I received. I don't mean to suggest that my parents are monstrous humans who have committed terrible personal crimes. They are simply individuals, like myself, who have been damaged as children. Upon becoming parents, they passed the damage onto their children, in this case, me.

I choose to share my story with you in the sincere hope that you may find some help or comfort in your own earnest search for working solutions to the problems facing you in your relationship. I include information about my addictions and the dysfunctional behavior of my family-of-origin because they are elements that contribute to my behavior in my relationship.

My mother became pregnant with me when she was eighteen and still unmarried. Her mother and grandmother used this circumstance to shame her. Her grandmother told her to leave the family house, and her mother withdrew a "contract" wherein my mother would have received $4,000 had she remained "pure" until the time she married. Her parents also informed her that she could not depend on them. She had to live entirely by her own means. This was the crowning event of my grandparents' shaming and scapegoating my mother throughout her childhood. In this spirit of shame and abandonment, my mother married my father and they moved to a tiny efficiency in the city.

In the spring of 1961 I was born, and one month later my parents moved to a small two-bedroom townhouse in the suburbs. During the following three years, we lived together as a family. My father finished his last year of college while working at night to support us. My mother prematurely ended her college career to work full-time housekeeping and childrearing. My parents had regular fraternity parties at the house (as a toddler I sometimes got drunk at these events). After my father began working days, my

107

mother felt more and more abandoned by my father's escalating drinking. He began to miss dinners and stayed out late drinking with increasing frequency. Finally, my mother consulted a doctor who identified my father's alcoholism. He made her aware that my father might or might not quit drinking and that she could choose to stay under those circumstances or leave. She chose to leave and my parents divorced just after I was three.

That year, my mother found a job as a Girl Friday; I began daycare, and we became the best of pals. One night my father visited. He showed me how to shake hands. I felt overjoyed that daddy had found his way home. You can imagine how I felt when he left again and I realized that his absence was intentional rather than by some accident. I may have been spared from the direct effects of parental alcoholism but I did experience the absence of my father as a result of his disease.

Roughly one year after my parents' divorce, my mother began dating a man who would become my stepfather a short while later. His son was only one day older than me. Initially, we were a happy family, but as time progressed, this man became more violent. I recall one night that my mother had taken me into her room as if to protect me and clutched me while screaming hysterically in fear as my stepfather beat on the door and yelled threats. I was terrified. Then a few months later, he brought a bowl of soup for me into my first grade classroom and tried to explain that he was taking my brother. I simply couldn't understand but I enjoyed the special attention. That afternoon, he left with my brother. My mother held me and cried as I watched them drive away.

From this point on, I began to experience grief over the absence of my family, but I didn't know how to express the pain and sadness and anger. I needed help, but as my mother's emotional needs had not been met as a child, she did not know how to help me with my needs. Instead, she used me to meet her needs. Therefore, because I could not express or release my pain, sadness, and so on, these feelings stayed inside me for many years. I had internalized them. I continued to internalize feelings when new emotional circumstances arose.

Carrying my emotional baggage was uncomfortable, so naturally I developed some tools to distract myself from these unprocessed feelings. I began to withdraw and I discovered, somewhat unconsciously, that isolating was more comfortable than socializing because I didn't create troubling emotional situations for myself. Reading lots of books disguised my withdrawal and provided me with another tool for emotional escape fantasy. Likewise, school work provided intellectual pursuits which were equally effective for shutting down my feelings.

I was six years old when my second family left. My mother and I once again became very close. We cuddled in bed on weekend mornings and I spent most of my mother's free time with her. Our neighbor's children brought their father's Playboy magazines to my backyard "fort." Looking at the nude women did not sexually arouse me, as I was seven years old;

however, I did experience immediate and intense mood changes. I felt excitement a quickening of my heartbeat and shortness of breath. I felt guilt and shame and curiosity. Only two years ago, I was finally able to recognize that this was the initial stage of my addiction to pornography.

When I was eight years old, my mother met a third man whom she married after a few months. I viewed this man and his attendant son and daughter with some suspicion. I did not trust that they cared enough about my mother and me to stay with us. Also, I noticed that this man drove a real wedge between my mother and me. Gone were our cuddly mornings and extra times spent with each other. Suddenly, I found myself in the back seat with two other children who were strangers to me with whom I was expected to share my time. I eventually began to accept these people and grew closer to them, but this marriage ended after eight months.

My mother was married and divorced one more time, for a total of four marriages and divorces, before I was sixteen. Between the third and fourth marriages, she dated numerous men and had two longer relationships, each lasting about a year. In between relationships and affairs, my mother used me to meet her partnership needs. We would be close when she had no partner, and I was abandoned when the partners came along. She used me as her surrogate spouse. My mother's behavior toward me became increasingly "boundaryless" as her sexual addiction progressed. She would use the bathroom with the door open, dress in front of me, and ask me to give her bodyrubs while she was nude. I would be shamed while giving her these massages during my adolescence, because she would tell me not to look at her genitals, while requesting me to rub her buttocks or legs. I did not realize that this behavior on my mother's part was incest until three years ago. Prior to this time, I only felt shame that by accident or curiosity, I had seen my mother's genitals. Through these experiences, I began to equate sex with love.

When I was fourteen years old, I began to drink on weekend evenings when my mother was out dating, which was almost every weekend. I drank between a half a pint to a pint of vodka each night. I also began smoking cigarettes. Here I launched my alcoholic career, with a brief interlude of social drinking the following year when I began to attend boarding school. I survived this year with tolerable grades, even though I felt that I was near my bursting point emotionally. During the summer, I started using illegal drugs. This was also the summer that I was raped by a man when I was hitchhiking.

The following school year I came apart. My alcohol, drug, and pornography use became nearly daily activities. My grades plummeted. I met a girl at school that year and fell head over heels in love. She practiced much of the same "come here, go away" behaviors as my mother, and much of the sexual promiscuity as well. I wanted to be monogamous, but she wanted an "open" relationship, so I acquiesced. At semester break, the school asked me to leave, instead of attempting to determine the cause of the precipitous drop in my grades, or providing me with help. I was crushed. When I came home, I learned that my mother had turned my bedroom into an office even though she had promised me that I would always have a place to come home to until I came of age. I slept on a couch in the family room and was also shamed about sleeping in the morning when employees were in the house. Then my mother put me in a psychiatric day-care center where they knew nothing about addiction, sexual abuse, or family dysfunction. This treatment was ineffective.

About this time, my father, whom I had only seen or heard from a few times in fourteen years, got sober and contacted my mother. My mother seized upon this opportunity to give custody of me to my father, even though he was in his first month of sobriety, and he made it clear that he could not care for me. For the next three years, I was shuttled between my father, my grandparents and my mother. As I had not been allowed to apply for a driver's license, I hitchhiked from my temporary homes to visit my high school girlfriend, and to go to bars. A number of times over these three years (ages sixteen through nineteen) I was picked up while hitchhiking by men who gave me alcohol and drugs in return for sex.

I had, during this time, a one-week and a three-week stay in psychiatric wards. These programs also knew nothing about sexual abuse, addiction, or family dysfunction. My shame deepened as I was treated by the psychiatric community as the "problem," rather than an indication of the problems in the family that needed to be resolved systemically. I kept dropping out of high school, as I could not handle the work, or anything else, for that matter. At one point, my father even took me to court as incorrigible.

I was put in a halfway house, and the staff informed my father that I needed more help than they could provide, but he did not get it for me. He kicked me out, and I went to live in a house owned by a man I did not know, but where I heard through friends that I could stay. It turned out that I was expected to pay for my rent with my body, which I did. I was not yet eighteen. Besides being raped for rent, I was also locked in the basement with a man I did not know and raped again in that house while friends of the owner watched through the windows. I got out of that situation and briefly lived with my mother, and then with my grandparents after I turned eighteen and my mother kicked me out. While I lived with my grandparents, I went to school for one semester, dropped out, and stole beer when I could in order to drink with my alcoholic friends.

I attempted to commit suicide by drinking half a bottle of rat poison in July of the year I turned nineteen. I almost died but was miraculously saved by my grandfather, who somehow discovered the empty bottle amidst the clutter in the very cluttered garage. I spent five weeks on a psychiatric unit, and then a year in long-term residential treatment for emotionally disturbed teenagers. In this treatment program, I was reintroduced to AA. The treatment program did not understand addiction, but they had one meeting a week on site, and I attended. (Mainly because I liked a pretty girl who was going to meetings!) I attained six months of continuous sobriety, which ended when the treatment program required me to find a place to live for my six month outpatient treatment. They offered me no help in finding a place to live, and so I went to live with my drinking buddies, as I had no idea of how to find a place to live other than with people I already knew. (The people who attended my AA meeting were residents on site.) After thirteen months of drinking hell, I called my grandmother in desperation and asked her to take me to a meeting. She did, and I have been sober for the ten years since.

In the past three years, I have discovered and begun to recover from other addictions. I have stopped using pornography, and have begun to take a teensy look at my money issues, which were created in childhood and exacerbated by the fact that my father did not contribute child support, so my mother and I lived near poverty quite often. I have begun to work with a therapist who is familiar with 12-Step programs, sexual abuse, and family dysfunction. I have started to grieve the loss of a safe family and childhood to feel the feelings I used drugs, pornography, alcohol, cigarettes, and more, to numb.

In my early sobriety, I desperately wanted to date women who were also sober and who were available to me sexually; because, as I associated sex with love, I wanted to be loved. I dated a few women in my early sobriety but did not get into a long term relationship until I was four years sober. I met a woman, and we had sex on our first date. I immediately leapt into the relationship with both feet. Within a month I was living with her. I assumed the role of caretaker, just as I had learned with my mother. We seemed to be doing well, but in my gut I began to recognize that I did not want to continue taking care of her financially and emotionally to my own detriment. I did not realize at the time that I was repeating the pattern I had learned with my mother. I began therapy and realized more and more that I wanted to leave. I didn't know that we could change our dynamics. I was unaware of RCA, and I didn't realize that we were acting out old family patterns that could be healed, so I left.

Just before I ended that relationship, I began to notice a woman in another 12-Step program who talked about ways that she was learning to take care of herself. I was impressed and I listened to her carefully in later meetings. She was also very attractive, so I really wanted to meet her and I hoped that she would like me. Beth agreed to join me for coffee at the local family restaurant. With a good deal of embarrassment, I recall that while trying to impress her, I poured my life story out to her as though I had no boundaries. I also made remarks that clearly indicated that I was in active sex addiction as well. When we parted and I asked her for a hug she replied, "I don't do men." I reeled with the realization that my behavior had been revolting and felt saddened that I had pushed Beth away. Later, I found that she only hugged men who she knew well and she hadn't found me so revolting that she wouldn't go out with me again. We seemed to be attracted to each other like sex-addicted magnets. Since I was still in a relationship, we didn't fully act on our mutual attraction, but we did engage in some inappropriate intrigue. Shortly after I ended my relationship, we were courting. I would like to say that we were and are a picture of perfect couple health, but truly, the lack of healthy coupleship models when we were young, and our absence of partnering skills, have often left us struggling in our relationship as we learn basic tools and behaviors.

Since we have been in RCA, we have gotten a real boost in the frequency with which we are relieved of our addictive relationship behaviors. We have learned new ways of interacting and communicating. Once we realized that we were in a relationship, we knew that we needed help. We sought help from a coupleship counselor. We have been seeing this counselor almost since the beginning of our relationship. We still consider that therapy essential to our relationship recovery, but it wasn't until we added RCA to our sources of help that our efforts really started to pay off consistently. Applying the steps to our relationship is not something we were taught how to do in our individual recovery programs. RCA has given us the tools we need to keep bringing the healing that we do in our individual recoveries back into the coupleship. We have been able to recognize the little child in each other and to remember more often that we are friends, not enemies, even in the middle of fights.

It has also been of great benefit to us to have the tools provided in the RCA literature. The reflections and the weekly inventory sheets have been very helpful, even though we have not gotten into the discipline of using them regularly.

Hearing other couples relate their problems, such as struggles with their addictive behaviors, fights, and so on, has been very healing for us. We no longer feel that we are so shameful, or completely unique. Likewise, sharing our difficult issues with other couples has been comforting and enlightening to us. We now know that our relationship is not hopeless. This has been a great relief to us. RCA has brought us closer; we are experiencing intimacy for the first time. We have come to believe that what is written in the AA Big Book applies to our RCA recovery; the promises can come true for us if we only work for them.

Daily Couple Reflections

Index

ও৩৯৯৩৯

REFLECTION NO. 1
Making Time For Intimacy

We live in a culture in which the average couple spends less than twenty-seven and a half minutes engaged in direct conversation together per week. Recovering people, however, know the price of neglected relationships. The old compulsions and obsessions drained our energy and occupied our time. In our pain and anger, we probably communicated even less than the meager national average. One of the gifts of recovery is the certain knowledge that what we wanted all along was intimacy. Our illness seduced us into taking care of our pain in unhealthy ways, as opposed to the closeness we could offer one another.

Our commitment today

Today we will work for the opportunities to connect with one another. We will attend to those moments when we are together. We will talk about whether we have enough time structured in the future. We will remember from our past experience that intimacy is an accumulation of little moments as well as large blocks of time.

My commitment today

Today I will remember that my past obsessions were a way to avoid my feelings and life choices and that what I really needed was support and nurturing.

ও৩৯৯৩৯

REFLECTION NO. 2
Need For Community

Couples experience more stress now than perhaps at any other time in history. For example, this is the first time in history that humankind has expected just two people to raise children. Parents in the eighteenth century had more childcare options that we routinely have now. In earlier times, extended family and friends were available for help when it was needed. Now, we live in neighborhoods and apartments in which we largely do not know others. Further, we move on the average of every three years, which is about the time it takes to become rooted in a community. Clearly, our culture does not support those of us in recovery who came from families already isolated and incapable of asking for help.

Our commitment today

Today we will acknowledge to each other our need for others to support our life as relationship partners. We need that support and community so that we do not return to being isolated from each other and the rest of the world. We will seek one firm course of action that we can take to add to our community.

My commitment today

Today I will remember that there are my partner's friends, there are my friends, and there are our friends together. All three are indispensable for recovery.

❧✦❧✦❧✦

REFLECTION NO. 3
CoupleShame

Many of us experience shame about our relationship; we think others would not want to be with us as a couple. We may be embarrassed about past behavior. We may still distrust being with others because we fear old behaviors might return. Or we may feel so shameful, we cannot believe that "good" people would enjoy us, accept our struggles, and share themselves with us. Sometimes we fear others will see realities about ourselves which we either do not perceive, or do not wish to admit to ourselves. Sometimes we fail to share these feelings with others.

Our commitment today

Today we will reflect on how we feel about being with others. Do we have shame about our relationship? What strengths do we have to offer others? What agreements or boundaries do we need to feel safe in "public?" Would it help for us to talk to other couples about our feelings?

My commitment today

Today I will work on accepting our progress as sufficient and focus on our strengths. I will comment aloud to my partner during the day about positive aspects of our being together.

ے9ﻮحﻮ9ﻮحﻮ9ﻮحﻮ

REFLECTION NO. 4
Couple Self-Concept

As individuals have self-concepts, couples have an "us" concept. How a couple perceives its relationship will profoundly affect its well-being. In our individual recoveries, we learned that how we talked about ourselves or to ourselves had a direct impact on our self-worth. Self-pity, self-blame, and self-judgment always added to the burden and worsened the situation. The same principle applies to relationships. When we judge each other or the relationship harshly, or indulge in another round of "ain't it awful being together," we remain stuck in the old patterns. Our recovery demands that we extend to our friendship that essential gentleness which was fundamental to forgiving ourselves.

Our commitment today

Today we will seek to treat gently our time together. We will accept the fact that intimacy is difficult, especially for recovering people. We will be forgiving of "us," and easy with one another. We will allow our sense of humor to be our guides.

My commitment today

I will not take myself too seriously. Rather I will look for ways to be good to myself and my partner. I will remind myself that I do not have the power necessary to fix instantly the things about which I am obsessive.

ے9ﻮحﻮ9ﻮحﻮ9ﻮحﻮ

REFLECTION NO. 5
Family-of-Origin

A relationship is a "blending of epics." Both partners carry within them the story of the previous generations. Recovering people coming from dysfunctional families often have bitter histories. Part of powerlessness is growing up in relationships where the only options were addiction or co-dependency. As we grow in recovery, we understand more fully the impact of our families on how we relate to others. Sadly, we also have to recognize how our distrust, terror and anger can easily be misplaced on our current partners, who do not deserve it. Part of our progress is to recognize that although we can no longer alter old family ties, we can do something about our current relationships.

Our commitment today

Today we will remind ourselves how far we have come from the old family pains. We will refuse to allow our addictive inheritances to interfere with how we are with one another now. One step we can take is to ask each other if something we are upset about represents contamination from the past.

My commitment today

Today I will be conscious of voices from my addictive past urging me toward destructive behavior with my partner in the present.

ৡড়ৡড়ৡড়

REFLECTION NO. 6
Spirituality and Vulnerability

Many people experience their spirituality as individuals in solitude. Still others experience spiritual connection in community--a church or Twelve-Step group, for example. We may find one-to-one spirituality more frightening because sharing our conscious contact is one of the most intimate things we can do. The risk to be spiritually vulnerable to a partner who knows us well is profoundly different from solitude. As with so many other risks in our recovery, the greater our vulnerability, the deeper our potential growth. Remember, we "came to believe that a power greater than ourselves could restore us to commitment and intimacy."

Our commitment today

Today we will ask each other what risks we are willing to take with one another spiritually. How do we implement the Second and Third Steps into our daily lives together? How prepared are we to turn our partnership over to a power greater than ourselves?

My commitment today

Today I will ask myself what new spiritual risk I am willing to take with my partner or in my partner's presence.

117

కళుకళుకళు

REFLECTION NO. 7
Support

One of the most difficult moments as a couple occurs when both partners are depleted and "over the edge" at the same time. Traditional wisdom has it that if you cannot get support from your partner, you should seek it from others individually. Another option exists. Part of recovery for the relationship is to develop a network of other couples who can be there for us during tough moments. Having such friendships in our lives will enhance our recovery if we develop them and call on our friends when we need them.

Our commitment today

Today we will talk about who in our network we can call when we are both overwhelmed. What kinds of excuses would we use to avoid calling them?

My commitment today

Today I will remember that building support for our relationship is another way of taking care of myself.

కళుకళుకళు

REFLECTION NO. 8
Partner-Blame

Blaming our partner is perhaps the most devastating dynamic available to addictive relationship partners. The dynamic becomes so familiar that we are unaware when we do it. Clues exist, however, to indicate when we are blaming. When we make absolute statements about the person such as, "you always do this" or "you are so..." or "you are such..." we are making blaming statements. If we critique the behavior ("I don't like this behavior") and not the person, we will be taking responsibility for what concerns us-- and not pushing all the responsibility to our partner.

Our commitment today

Today we will contract to talk about our concerns respectfully. We will discuss how we can affirm each other and still have our issues heard.

My commitment today

Today I will remember that how I talk about something can be as important as the problem I wish to discuss.

ৡ৯ৡ৯ৡ৯

REFLECTION NO. 9
Unresolvable Issues

Every couple has an issue that appears to unresolvable. No matter how often it has been talked about, or what solutions have been tried, the problem did not go away. Here is where the program can really help. In our addiction and codependency, we tried harder to solve a problem only to have the situation worsen. However, when we admitted our powerlessness and sought help, we were able to make progress. Similarly, part of a First Step as a couple is to recognize powerlessness over that "unresolvable issue." By admitting the issue, a couple can gain support form others who have experienced similar patterns in their recovery. The starting point is to remember that our illness is a family illness.

Our commitment today

Today we will discuss one of our unresolvable issues and commit to seeking support. We will remind each other that we are not alone in having difficult issues which refuse to go away.

My commitment today

Today I will be patient with our partnership and remember that my powerlessness persists in my relationships as well.

ৡ৯ৡ৯ৡ৯

REFLECTION NO. 10
Stress

Family researchers have long noted that marital satisfaction declines markedly in most couples when their children become teenagers and returns when those adolescents become adults. The lesson to be learned is that ongoing stress takes a toll on the quality of relationship-life people have. Such stressors are unavoidable; we cannot change, for example, the turmoil that emerging adulthood brings to our children. What we can do is seek support from others to minimize the impact on the vitality of our life together.

Our commitment today

Today we will remember the serenity prayer: we will recognize those things over which we have no power, and change the things we can. We will pray today for the wisdom to know the difference.

My commitment today

Today I will support my partner by recognizing our limits. I will remember gentleness and simplicity.

ৼৡৼৡৼৡ

REFLECTION NO. 11
Struggles and Understanding

A child takes her mother's shoes off and plays with them. She struggles to get them back on her mom's feet. She experiments, testing various ways to get them to fit. What started as play evolves into a challenge and a struggle. She works hard to master how shoes and feet fit together. Her parent, being wise about learning, resists the impulse to show her how they fit. She knows that it is more important for the child to develop the capability to make sense out of her world than to know about shoes. So she watches patiently with care and, at times, amusement. She reflects about whether this is how God watches our relationships--as we try to make things "fit:" patient, wise, caring, and sometimes amused.

Our commitment today

Today we will remember that our struggle to make things "fit" is not only to figure out the puzzle, but also to add to our ability to understand our world. Today we will share examples of how being with each other has expanded our perceptions. We can play with the fantasy about how God looks upon our efforts to "fit."

My commitment today

Today I will ask my Higher Power for the wisdom to appreciate my relationships and all the accompanying struggles as central to my ability to see purpose in life.

ঙ৯ঙ৯ঙ৯

REFLECTION NO. 12
Interdependency

Nature teaches about growth in many ways. We need only to walk through a forest or desert to see the interdependency among creatures, plants, and environment. We can gaze at a body of water from ocean to small pond to marvel at the complex relationships that make for thriving growth. The urge to be together for safety, comfort, reproduction, and play is one of the fundamental driving forces of the universe. We need to reflect on how being a couple is part of a total ecology and grand design. We can keep perspective on overwhelming issues when we see that our progress is shared by all of creation. Our efforts to connect as a couple draw upon those same sources of strength which routinely beat the odds.

Our commitment today

Today we will make an effort to connect with our roots as a couple by reflecting on nature. If possible we will arrange today or soon to be in an environment where we can sense together that energy which renews the world.

My commitment today

Today I will focus on my senses and how I experience nature in my life. I will report awareness of being an organism in this world to my partner.

ঙ৯ঙ৯ঙ৯

REFLECTION NO. 13
Despair

We all can reflect on moments of despair when our lives had totally unraveled. Our pain came either from tragic circumstances beyond our control or from our own choices. Yet our commitment to continue faltered because life seemed hopeless. Our recovery teaches us that these low points actually served as gifts in our lives. We changed for the better. The losses we experienced actually gave us a new life, with new wisdom. As couples we witness for partners our capacity to transform personal discouragement into individual depth.

Our commitment today

Today we will each share a despairing moment that deepened us as persons. We will remind ourselves that extreme difficulty is part of the renewing process and that we shall have such moments again. We can prepare by strengthening our partnership and by discussing what we need from one another when facing despair.

My commitment today

Today I will share a memory of how my partner helped me when I was despairing.

༚ ༝ ༚ ༝ ༚ ༝

REFLECTION NO. 14
Sensuality

Sensuality is fundamental to sexuality. How we notice our environment--how we see it, hear it, touch it, smell it, and taste it--is fundamental to our total experience of life. Both our sexuality and our sensuality give basic vitality to our relationship. But if we do not attend to our senses, our sexuality is diminished. As recovering persons, we know that we need to stay in the present as opposed to the tormented past or the uncertain future. Our senses are the gateway to the present. More than stopping to smell the roses, sensuality is a direct path to spirituality. Being in touch with our senses will help us to be present for one another both spiritually and sexually.

Our commitment today

Today we will talk about how sensually aware we are. We will focus on simple ways be be sensually present for one another. We can notice the food we eat, the beauty of a tree, the grace of a swallow's flight, the light of a new moon, or the color of a child's eyes.

My commitment today

Today I will seize life by heeding what my senses tell me. I will make a special effort to notice what is attractive about my partner and talk about it.

૯ઝ૯ઝ૯ઝ

REFLECTION NO. 15
Accepting Help

Recovering people have difficulty accepting help. Our reluctance stems from early life experiences. We were disappointed and hurt when help was necessary but not given. We grieve promises of help that never materialized. We resent obligation. For whatever reason, we decided to go it alone and not rely on others. But in that commitment we became further vulnerable to addiction and codependency. We needed assistance and found relief in our obsessions. Total couple recovery requires a deep commitment to acceptance of help from each other and from other couples.

Our commitment today

Today we will ask ourselves how well we accept help from each other and how well we accept help as a couple. What specific needs do we have at this moment for which we resist asking for help?

My commitment today

Today I will remember that self-sufficiency and independence are not the same and that part of self-determination is to be free to ask for help.

૯ઝ૯ઝ૯ઝ

REFLECTION NO. 16
Healthy Lifestyle

Recovering from addictive illnesses requires a couple's commitment to a totally healthy lifestyle. Food, exercise, and rest all become options to be explored to enhance healthy living. Sometimes the choices present significant issues for couples, as when a partner smokes or decides to be a vegetarian. Comfortable resolutions of these issues is one of the most basic elements of recovery, but sadly many of us simply let our lifestyles happen. In an increasingly health-conscious culture, we may feel guilty but only make futile attempts at change. Being of like mind on lifestyle changes means having your partner's support. From a recovery point of view, emotional well-being has a profound impact on physical well-being.

Our commitment today

Today we will ask each other how comfortable we are with our physical well-being. Do we need to set aside time to really talk through some changes? What pride can we take in how our lifestyle supports recovery?

My commitment today

Today I will think about my role as a lifestyle partner. As part of my weekly inventory, I will think about ways I do not contribute to a healthy lifestyle and what gifts of health my partner has given me.

❦❧❦❧❦❧

REFLECTION NO. 17
Perspective

When a child is ten years old, the passage of a year seems like an eternity. Given that one year out of ten is a full ten percent of that young person's life, it is a long time. As an adult, the years start to rush by and seem shorter. One year at the age of forty is only two and a half percent of your life. The adult's perception shifts because the same amount of time is less by comparison. Combine the perception shift, with the pressure of adult responsibilities, and time becomes even more elusive. Couples also experience a diminished sense of time the longer they are together. Recovering people, however, need to regain the time perspective of the ten-year-old, when the world was fresh and full of wonder. They start a day at a time.

Our commitment today

Today we will talk about how we would spend the day if we were both ten years old. Then we will reflect on what that means for us in living the program today.

My commitment today

Today I will connect with the child within me so that I may reclaim the enthusiasm, earnestness, and playfulness of myself. I will pray that I remain as open to the world as a ten-year-old.

❦❧❦❧❦❧

REFLECTION NO. 18
Openness and Acceptance

In every relationship, each partner comes to realizations that are difficult to admit to the other. Simply, it is that raw exposure of being fully known

124

by the other that fills us with fear. Since we come from the shame of addiction and codependency, an additional vulnerability exists. Something admitted to a partner could someday be used against us in a relapse of the old battles of right and wrong. Another way to think about sharing an insight with a partner is to see it as an invitation to the other to a renewed life in recovery. Remember: admitting something to your partner does not have to be graceful, articulate, or fully thought-out in order to be inviting. The half-understood, the dead end, and the elusive perception can be clarified simply by sharing.

Our commitment today

Today we will reflect on how open we are to admitting to each other the difficult things about ourselves. Do we have an accepting climate in which we feel free to admit to each other our most secret fears about ourselves?

My commitment today

Today I will inventory any admissions I have withheld from my partner. If I have something I am unsure about sharing, I will check it out with others in my program.

✍ ✍ ✍ ✍ ✍ ✍

REFLECTION NO. 19
Intimacy and Risk-Taking

Intimacy is an "inventure," meaning it is an internal adventure complete with high risk, excitement, and discovery. Many people want the excitement and the discovery without taking the risk. Recovery forces risk-taking, however, which is why the blessings of intimacy are available to recovering people. We are not talking about the Indiana Jones style of addictive life in which we took risks to stave off one disaster after another. Rather we are talking about the frontiers of oneself and of each other in which there are rewards for exploring new territory. There are the risks of new levels of honesty with each other, or of learning to play with each other, of reaching out in new ways sexually with each other, or of sharing creativity with each other. As addiction was always there as a predictable way to kill pain and emptiness, the intimacy "inventure" is always there for us to renew ourselves.

Our commitment today

Today we will have a candid discussion about new risks we can take together. To what new "inventure" are we willing to commit today?

My commitment today

Today I will reflect on the spiritual quest involved in risk-taking. How can I use risk-taking as part of a Third Step in which I trust my Higher Power?

ৡ৽ৡ৽ৡ৽

REFLECTION NO. 20
Witnessing our Partner's Struggles

Many of us have lived tough lives. Unfortunately, recovery does not ensure that difficult times will not recur. In that sense the First Step is an introductory course to the wisdom of the serenity prayer: we must understand that there is much in our lives over which we will remain powerless. We must incorporate that understanding into our relationships. For every couple there will be moments when one partner will flounder and experience deep pain while all the other can do is witness the suffering. At that point, the Steps become vital guides to how to be respectful toward each other. First, there is a deep acknowledgment of personal powerlessness and admitting the limits of your help. Next is an act of faith that a Higher Power is at work for your partner and for you. Finally, the support of your fellowship can support you in your witnessing role.

Our commitment today

Today we will share a memory when each could only witness the other's struggle. We will re-commit to enduring those difficult transactions.

My commitment today

Today I will remember how the Steps can be guidelines in respecting my partner.

ৡ৽ৡ৽ৡ৽

REFLECTION NO. 21
Keeping our Reality

Relationship partners can share in delusion. When neither partner faces a harsh reality, they are vulnerable again to the old obsessions. Healthy relationship means deep dedication to reality, whatever the cost. Twelve-Step wisdom has always urged us to go to "any lengths" to keep our realities. So when we face issues like aging parents, addicted teenagers, limited finances, or unhealthy lifestyles, we need to be willing to raise possible

126

problems, and then take the action to confirm or deny the existence of those problems. The last thing needed in recovery is shared denial.

Our commitment today

Today we will share wonders and worries about problems we may not have acknowledged. To what lengths will we go to keep our reality?

My commitment today

Fighting denial starts with listening to my inner voice that tells me something is uncomfortable or not right. I will recognize that voice by sharing my concerns with my partner.

෬ඁ෨ඁ෬ඁ෨ඁ෬ඁ෨ඁ

REFLECTION NO. 22
Conflict

If you love someone and wish to be intimate with them, you have to be prepared to fight with them. Arguing is one of the most positive forms of intimacy, and anger is one of the most significant of the relationship gifts. To quarrel confidently with your partner indicates that you value and respect your partner as an adult who can handle it. To avoid conflict is to diminish your partner, leave issues unresolved, and constrict all feelings, including joy, tenderness and care. In the old days, we had battles over right and wrong. We escalated issues into crises during which our obsession would thrive. We preferred dramatic exits to being clear about our feelings. Now we avoid self-righteousness and blame, and we strive for honesty and accuracy. We work for resolution, not crisis. We do not damage each other. We leave out extraneous issues. We do not abandon each other. And through this we learned peace together.

Our commitment today

Today we will share our insecurities about fighting and how we will support each other in conflict.

My commitment today

Today I am not going to avoid conflict. I will be real with people and set aside my fears about the reactions of others, especially my partner.

౭ఌ৯౭ఌ৯౭ఌ৯

REFLECTION NO. 23
Tolerating Pain

Because of our history, we have learned to tolerate pain. Most people who experience pain make changes to reduce or eliminate it. A basic principle for self-care and self-respect demands that we take action. For those of us who have relied on addictive obsession to cope with pain, confronting our tolerance of pain becomes difficult. We are used to hurting. Physically, we ignore tiredness, full bladders, soreness and discomfort. We can sustain personal emptiness and shame. In our relationships, we bury our feelings, allowing disrespect to continue. As couples, we "adjust" to pain. Intolerable situations exist in which both partners simply try harder. Recovery means both partners working together to develop intolerance of pain.

Our commitment today

Today we will talk of ways we hurt together. We will decide on which steps to take action, and when we will take those steps.

My commitment today

Today I will tune into any pain to which I may have become accustomed. I will make an effort to report this to my partner.

౭ఌ৯౭ఌ৯౭ఌ৯

REFLECTION NO. 24
Committing to Physical Health

Recovery requires a commitment to physical health. For years, we ignored our bodies and nearly destroyed one of our best bridges to emotional well-being. Solid exercise and eating well are proven contributors to psychological health. We need to be good consumers of health information. We can make changes that would improve our quality of life. The cooperation and support of our partners, however, is key. In our codependency, we had an investment in the other's illness. Now, in recovery, we invest in our partner's health and our own health. Couples can do much together as well as mutually support each other in a "training program" for recovery.

Our commitment today

Today we will talk about what we can do together to improve our physical health. Do we need more information? How can we support each other?

128

My commitment today

Today I will think about how I feel about my body and how I can live my commitment to physical health.

REFLECTION NO. 25
Acceptance and Healing

In many ways, an intimate relationship parallels a Fifth Step. Part of the healing of a Fifth Step is to be fully known--both strengths and liabilities-- and accepted. Relationships heal when we accept each other's strengths and liabilities. Problems emerge when we control, shame, limit or abandon our partners either because we find a threatening strength or a disappointing liability. Honesty between two people does not mean that one or the other is diminished. Rather, honesty reflects a fundamental acceptance of our limitations and support for our humanness.

Our commitment today

Today we will share our acceptance of each other by admitting ways in which we each try to be perfect.

My commitment today

Today I will be gentle with myself by accepting my imperfections. I will challenge that part of myself which says nothing is good enough.

REFLECTION NO. 26
Faithfulness

Faithfulness starts with fidelity to oneself. You can rely upon those who know what they want, say what they mean, and do what they say. People who are true to themselves make trustworthy commitments. Those who make decisions on the basis of what would look good, or what the other person wants, lose themselves in the process. We as couples need to understand that to be faithful means to be clear about who we are. No betrayal exists when nothing has been misrepresented; we are faithful to others when we are true to ourselves.

Our commitment today

Today we will share with each other an example of something we absolutely trust about the other.

My commitment today

Today I will notice when I am not being true to myself. Am I trying to please others at the expense of who I am?

❧❧❧❧❧❧

REFLECTION NO. 27
Powerlessness

Most of us can remember times when we were upset and in turmoil. With the passage of time, however, we put these periods in perspective. We realize that the pain we experienced was necessary for us to grow. Or we might recognize that our self-righteousness and indignation was an exercise in blaming others for what we had brought on ourselves. Surely we recognized that we spent needless emotional energy feeling shameful. The program of recovery reminds us that much exists over which we have no power, that we need to take responsibility for ourselves, and that there is a higher power we can trust. As partners committed to a 12-Step process together, we can help each other take those lessons about our painful past and apply them to a balanced and serene present.

Our commitment today

Today we can make a pact with each other about how to support each other when we get upset.

My commitment today

Today I will keep in mind the lessons of former desperate situations. I will think of one example and reflect on what I learned from that experience.

ᕉᖇᕉᖇᕉᖇ

REFLECTION NO. 28
Mutual Respect

When relationships end, both partners are likely to say, "I didn't feel respected." Two very significant questions are often overlooked. First, did I act respectably? Were my behavior and attitudes consistently straight-forward and respectable? And second, was I respectful? Did I avoid shaming, abusive, and inappropriate treatment of my partner? Was my anger constructive or destructive? When issues existed, did I work to ensure that my partner did not feel diminished by our process? Acting respectably and being respectful create an integrity that commands respect.

Our commitment today

Today we will re-commit to mutual respect.

My commitment today

Today I ask myself if I have been respectable and respectful in my relationship. If I am unsure, I will contact a close friend and ask for feedback.

ᕉᖇᕉᖇᕉᖇ

REFLECTION NO. 29
Equality

Many couples start off looking for equality by searching for what they have in common. True equality, however, starts by discovering the strengths in differences. The differences between partners expand the options available, and the relationship is stronger. Equality emerges when differences become assets and sources of new options, versus irritants and sources of shame. Equality rests on respect for the strength in the other's differences.

Our commitment today

Today we share a difference that each of us respects in the other.

My commitment today

Today I will acknowledge to myself a difference in my partner that I find irritating and work to see how that difference might become a strength.

ى‌ڡ‌ى‌ڡ‌ى‌ڡ

REFLECTION NO. 30
Renewal and Risk-Taking

Relationships renew through risk taking. Couples who do new things together continue to rediscover their attraction for each other. They also find new perspectives on each other. Recovery presents many opportunities to take risks: new ways of being together, new strategies for sharing, new levels of honesty, new people, and new ways to support. Among the risks, the greatest is for partners to share vulnerability with each other. Risk always feels new and unsettling, so we feel dependent and inexperienced. As recovering people, we know we have problems with dependency. By sharing with each other the vulnerability we feel about our risk-taking, our opportunities for intimacy and support become exponential.

Our commitment today

Today we will assess our current level of risk-taking. Are we doing enough to keep the process of renewal alive?

My commitment today

Today I will share, with my partner, my vulnerability around risks I am now taking.

Notes